ELITE S

EDITOR: MART

British Forces in Zululand 1879

Text by IAN KNIGHT

Colour plates by RICHARD SCOLLINS

OSPREY PUBLISHING LONDON

Published in 1991 by
Osprey Publishing Ltd
59 Grosvenor Street, London, W1X 9DA
© Copyright 1991 Osprey Publishing Ltd

All rights reserved. Apart from any fair dealing for the purpose of private study, research, criticism or review, as permitted under the Copyright Designs and Patents Act, 1988, no part of this publication may be reproduced, stored in a retrieval system, or transmitted in any form or by any means, electronic, electrical, chemical, mechanical, optical, photocopying, recording or otherwise, without the prior permission of the copyright owner. Enquiries should be addressed to the Publishers.

British Library Cataloguing in Publication Data
Knight, Ian 1956–
  British forces in Zululand 1879. – (Elite series, 32).
  1. Great Britain. Army, history
  I. Title II. Series
  355.00941

ISBN 1-85532-109-2

Filmset in Great Britain
Printed through Bookbuilders Ltd, Hong Kong

Author's Note

I have found fellow enthusiasts of the Anglo-Zulu War to be unfailingly generous with the fruits of their individual researches, and this book has proved no exception. That acknowledged master of British colonial campaign dress, Michael Barthorp, helped fill some of the yawning gaps in my knowledge, and John Thomson's meticulous analysis of contemporary photographs was also of vital importance. Angus Konstam of the Royal Armouries shared his expertise in the field of 19th century rocketry and greatly eased my study of contemporary small arms. Ian Castle unselfishly allowed me access to his definitive notes on the Natal Volunteers, and, as ever, Claire Colbert's help with the photographic copying was invaluable. My thanks to them all.

Dedicated to two fellow travellers, Ian and 'The Chief'.

Artist's Note

Readers may care to note that the original paintings from which the colour plates in this book were prepared are available for private sale. All reproduction copyright whatsoever is retained by the publisher. All enquiries should be addressed to:
  Richard Scollins
  14 Ladywood Road,
  Ilkeston,
  Derbyshire
The publishers regret that they can enter into no correspondence upon this matter.

For a catalogue of all books published by Osprey Military please write to:

The Marketing Manager, Consumer Catalogue Department
Osprey Publishing Ltd, 59 Grosvenor Street, London, W1X 9DA

British Forces in Zululand 1879

The Zulu War

On 4 March, 1878 at King William's Town, British Kaffraria, Gen. Sir Arthur Cunynghame handed over supreme command of the British forces in southern Africa to his successor, Lt. Gen. Sir Frederic Thesiger. It was hardly a plum job. It was a fact of Imperial life that commanders in the Colonies were expected to achieve the maximum result with a minimal expense of resources, and southern Africa was going through a troublesome period of its history.

A war against the Xhosa people—the Ninth, and last, Cape Frontier War—was about to enter its final phase of dismal skirmishing, but across the region the African population was restless. The Basotho, upset by the attempts of Cape authorities to disarm them, were stirring, and one chief, Moorosi, was already moving towards confrontation. In 1877, as part of its Confederation policy—an attempt to rationalise its political and economic interests in the area—Britain had annexed and occupied the bankrupt Transvaal, the most inward-looking and Anglophobe of the Boer Republics. The Boers had reacted with sullen resentment, and a steady stream of troops were despatched across the monotonous 'high-veld' to garrison the more significant settlements. With the Transvaal had come a festering border dispute with the Pedi Chief Sekhukhune, which threatened to drag Britain into yet another small African war.

Yet none of these problems can have been uppermost in Thesiger's mind as 1878 wore on, since his political master, the High Commissioner, Sir Henry Bartle Frere, had another more pressing task for him to consider. Frere was convinced that one solution to the complex problems which beset the region was to overthrow the last powerful independent black kingdom bordering British possessions—the Zulu kingdom of King Cetshwayo kaMpande.

A prospective war with the Zulus posed Thesiger a number of clear strategic questions. The aggressive intent was all Britain's: Cetshwayo had remained on the political defensive, and was keen to avoid a confrontation. Thesiger would therefore have to take the war across the border of Colonial Natal and wage it in Zululand. Yet Zululand was a vast and difficult country; it covered some 15,000 square miles, most of it rolling downland dropping in a series of terraces from inland heights to a sub-tropical belt bordering the Indian Ocean. It was well-watered, but its majestic river systems had cut many deep gorges on their passages through the

Lieutenant-General Sir Frederic Augustus Thesiger, 2nd Baron Chelmsford, the British commander in the Anglo-Zulu War. He is wearing his campaign uniform of blue patrol jacket and riding breeches. The helmet puggaree was not authorised for use in South Africa, but does seem to have been worn by senior officers. (S. Bourquin)

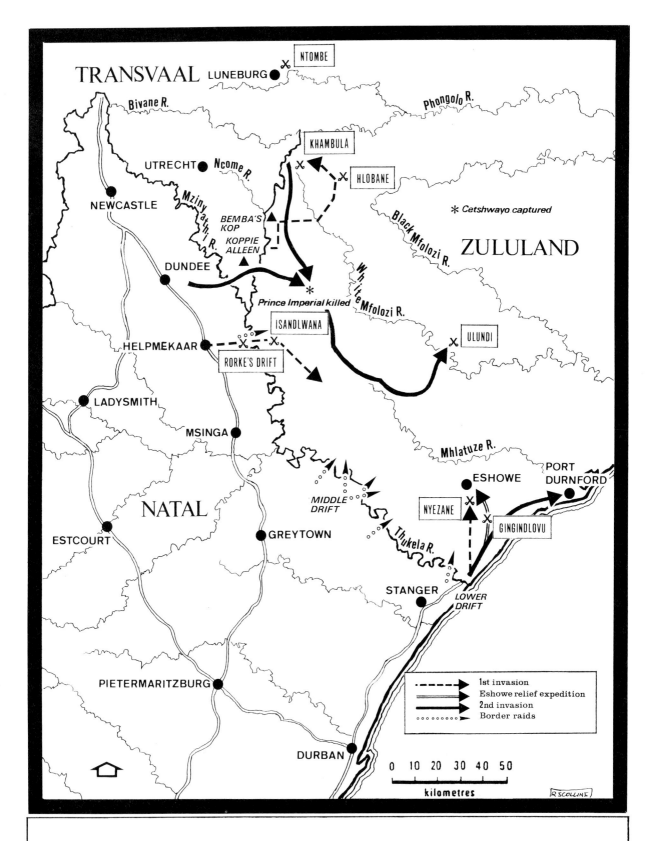

The British Invasion of Zululand · 1879

hills. Much of it was covered in bush or forest, large tracts of it were unmapped, and there were only a few traders' wagon tracks to serve as roads. The border with Natal was over 200 miles long, marked by the Mzinyathi (Buffalo) and Thukela Rivers, which might be crossed at dozens of points by the Zulu army, but which remained very real obstacles to more encumbered European troops.

Thesiger's initial strategy called for five separate columns to be massed at points stretching from the mouth of the Thukela in the south-east up to the Transvaal in the north. Yet he had remarkably few troops available for such an enterprise. Six infantry battalions were already in South Africa, mopping up the Cape Frontier or garrisoning the Transvaal—the 2/3rd, 1/13th, 1st and 2nd/24th, 80th and 90th—and another, the 88th, was arriving in a steady trickle from Mauritius. There were two artillery batteries available, N/5 and 11/7; a solitary company of Royal Engineers; and an absurdly small Transport staff, to whom the enormous burden of ensuring that supplies were ferried in the wake of the advance would fall. There were no regular cavalry, only two squadrons of Mounted Infantry and a handful of small Volunteer units drawn from the settler community. Natal's large black population, for the most part hostile to the Zulus, was a potential source of levies, but clearly manpower remained in short supply. Thesiger appealed to the home government for reinforcements; but the Colonial Office did not support Frere's war-mongering, and the general was sent only two more infantry battalions (the 2/4th and 99th) and two Engineer companies (2nd and 5th).

By late 1878 Frere had manipulated a diplomatic crisis with the Zulus. Thesiger—who succeeded to the title Lord Chelmsford on the death of his father in October—completed his plans. He retained the concept of five columns, but reduced two of them to defensive border garrisons, leaving three to act as an invasion force to converge on the Zulu capital at Ulundi. Three advancing columns were much easier to supply than two; they risked diluting Chelmsford's greatest asset—the massed firepower of his infantry battalions—but allowed the Zulus little room for manoeuvre in the counter-strike against Natal.

The Right Flank Column (No. 1) was comman-

Col. Henry Evelyn Wood, commander of the Right Flank Column, in his service dress. He is wearing the officers' undress frock of the 90 LI (buff collar and regimental badge). His rank is indicated by the braid on his sleeve and by the star and crown badges on his collar. His helmet bears the splendid 1878 pattern plate and fittings, although sketches of him in the field show him to be wearing a less conspicuous dyed helmet with no fixtures. (Royal Collection)

ded by Col. Charles Pearson of the 3rd Foot, and collected at the Lower Drift, just inland from the mouth of the Thukela. Number 2 Column, consisting largely of African troops under Lt. Col. Anthony Durnford RE, would be based on the Natal side of the Middle Drift of the Thukela. The Centre Column (No. 3) would cross over from its supply depot at the Rorke's Drift mission station on the Mzinyathi. It was commanded by Lt. Col. Richard Glynn of the 24th, but accompanied by the general himself, and was intended as the main striking arm. The Left Flank Column (No. 4) was commanded by Col. H. Evelyn Wood, 90th LI, and would cross the Ncome (Blood) River into Zululand from the Transvaal. The final column, No. 5, under Col. Hugh Rowlands, 34th Foot, would remain further north on the Transvaal border, where it could keep an eye not only on the Zulus but on the Boers and Pedi as well.

The timing of the campaign would also be significant. Most of the rain in Natal and Zululand falls in the summer months—December, January and February. During that time the rivers are swollen and tracks can easily be churned to greasy quagmires; but the grass is tall and fresh, and there would be a minimal chance of the Zulus lighting grass fires. In 1878 the whole region was suffering from a drought, so Chelmsford might have had the best of both worlds; in addition, the late rains were delaying the harvests, and there was the possibility that the Zulus might be distracted in a summer campaign by the need to gather their crops. Accordingly, Frere timed his showdown with Cetshwayo to give Chelmsford all the benefits of a summer campaign.

General Sir Garnet Wolseley, who superseded both Chelmsford and Frere at the end of the war, in the uniform he wore as Special Commissioner for Southern Africa, with both civil and military powers. (Author's Collection)

Officers of the Buffs photographed in Natal shortly before the start of the campaign. They are wearing either the blue patrol jacket or the scarlet frock, and forage caps or foreign service helmets. The brass spikes and chin-chains visible here were not worn on campaign (Canterbury City Museum)

Zulu representatives were summoned to a meeting at the Lower Drift and presented with an ultimatum with which, Frere knew, they could not possibly comply. The time allotted for compliance with the ultimatum expired on 11 January 1879. During the last few weeks the troops were marched into position and the stores amassed. A small Naval contingent from HMS Active was landed to join Pearson's column. No news came from Cetshwayo. The war began.

* * *

From the start, it did not go well. The drought finally broke, and Chelmsford's columns began their advance amongst torrential downpours. The general had voiced a fear that he might have trouble forcing the Zulus to fight, but he had underestimated his enemy. Once King Cetshwayo realised that he could not avoid a confrontation he had taken steps to deal with the British strategy. Local elements from his army were ordered to harass the flanking columns, while the main Zulu strike force was despatched to confront Chelmsford. By 20 January the two armies were drawing close to one another. Chelmsford misread the situation, and on the 21st split his force, leaving one portion in the camp at Isandlwana while marching out himself with the other. As an afterthought he scribbled a note to Durnford asking him to bring his column up to support the camp. Durnford's men had scarcely entered the camp on the 22nd when they stumbled upon the main Zulu impi, and precipitated a battle which ended in the massacre of the camp's defenders. The defence of the depot at Rorke's Drift by a single company of the 2/24th against attacks by the Zulu reserve could not obscure the magnitude of the disaster. Chelmsford's initial plan was smashed; in the aftermath he could do little but fall back on Natal, try to shore up his defences, and hope the Zulus did not launch a further foray into Natal.

The flank columns were left high and dry. Pearson had also been engaged on the 22nd—he had broken a Zulu attempt to block his advance on the hills above the Nyezane River—and had pushed forward to the deserted mission station at Eshowe. Here he dug in to await developments, while the Zulus gathered in increasing numbers in the hills around him, laying him under siege. Only Evelyn Wood was free in the north, and he relentlessly harried the Zulu clans in his vicinity.

Yet the main Zulu army did not cross into Natal. Isandlwana had exhausted them, and the king still hoped to win political advantage by waging a defensive war. Chelmsford was allowed the respite he needed to regroup. The home government, embarrassed by Isandlwana, sought to restore British honour by despatching more reinforcements than even Chelmsford had asked for. He received six further infantry battalions (2/21st, 57th, 58th, 3/60th, 91st and 94th); two full artillery batteries (M/6 and N/6); a company of Engineers (30th); three companies of the Army Service Corps (3, 4 and 5); and a company of the Army Hospital Corps. Where before he had no cavalry except what he could scrape together locally, now he was sent the 17th (Duke of

The blue patrol jacket and forage cap: 2nd Lt. Macarthy of the 4th Regiment. The badge on the forage cap is the number '4' surmounted by the 'Lion of England'. (King's Own Regimental Museum)

Officers of the 88th Regiment (Connaught Rangers) at Fort Pearson, Lower Drift, prior to the second invasion. This picture shows something of the variety of officers' service dress; Lt. Col. Hopton, centre, is wearing an OR's frock, as are the officers on either end of the front row. The two on either side of Hopton are wearing officers' frocks, and one has buttoned canvas or leather leggings. Patrol jackets are also in evidence, and headgear is the glengarry or forage cap. (National Army Museum)

Cambridge's Own) Lancers and the 1st (King's) Dragoon Guards. In addition there were drafts to make good his losses, miscellaneous support services, more Naval contingents, and no less than four major-generals.

As the troops arrived, so Chelmsford began to reassert control of the military stalemate. In March he moved to relieve Eshowe. Ordering his commanders along the border to make what diversionary attacks they could, he crossed the Thukela once more at the Lower Drift, and on 2 April defeated a Zulu force sent to confront him at Gingindlovu. Eshowe was relieved the next day, and within a week Chelmsford had brought his men back into Natal. In the meantime another decisive battle had already taken place at the other end of the country. Cetshwayo, too, had regrouped his forces, and this time sent them against Wood's column. Wood's intelligence reports had included rumours of their advance, but nevertheless Wood had decided to press ahead with an attack, timed to support Chelmsford, on the Zulu mountain stronghold of Hlobane. The attack, on 28 March, was badly co-ordinated, and turned into a rout on the appearance of the main Zulu army. Wood's men were only able to extricate themselves with heavy losses. The next day, however, the Zulu force attacked Wood's fortified camp at Khambula, and was driven off after hours of heavy fighting.

The battle of Khambula was the turning point of the war. The Zulus had attacked confident that, after Isandlwana, the British were no match for them, and they had been severely defeated. It was clear to the king and his generals that the war could not be won. Chelmsford was now in a position to begin his invasion afresh, making the most of his new resources. His new plan involved a much stronger column, designated the First Division, advancing from the Lower Drift and up the coastal lowlands. A second column, the Second Division, would cross into Zululand several miles north of Rorke's Drift and, skirting Isandlwana, cut across to join the old Centre Column's planned line of advance. Along the way it would affect a juncture with Wood's Column, now redesignated the Flying Column. The First Division was intended largely as support for a combined push by the Second Division and Flying Column.

The advance began in May, slowly groping forward, establishing small stone or earthwork forts every few miles to guard the supplies and the convoys that laboriously trundled back and forward to fetch them. There was constant skirmishing, but the Zulu army did not commit itself until Chelmsford finally reached Ulundi. Here, on 4 July, he formed his troops up in a huge hollow rectangle, and watched with satisfaction as the Zulu charges dashed themselves hopelessly against a hail of artillery and volley fire.

Chelmsford's conduct of the war was not without its critics, and the home government had at last lost patience, sending out Gen. Sir Garnet Wolseley to replace him. But Chelmsford had snatched his victory before Wolseley could reach the front, and by the time Sir Garnet arrived there was little to do beyond supervising the capture of Cetshwayo and suppressing the last patches of Zulu resistance. The Dragoons ran the king to earth in a remote hideaway in northern Zululand in August and led him away to exile; and at the beginning of September Wolseley imposed a settlement on Zululand and began to withdraw. By the end of the month the evacuation was complete.

According to the official record, during the campaign 76 officers and 1,007 men had died in action, together with 604 black auxiliaries, though this figure is a substantial underestimate. Thirty-seven officers, 206 men and 57 auxiliaries were

Rank distinction, infantry officers' undress frock. The braid is that of a major; note the looped 'bullet-hole' braid. (Author's Collection)

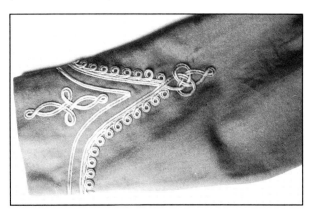

Infantry officers' forage cap, showing the oak-leaf braid and button design on top. A regimental badge and numeral would have been worn on the front. (Author's Collection)

wounded, and 17 officers and 330 men died of disease. A further 99 officers and 1,286 men were invalided 'from the command for causes incidental to the campaign'. The total cost of the war was estimated at the time as £5,230,323.

Perhaps 7,000 Zulus had been killed in war, and countless hundreds more wounded.

Infantry

The Cardwell Reforms

The standard battlefield tactical unit of the 1870s was not the regiment, but the infantry battalion. Since Edward Cardwell had become Secretary of State for War in Gladstone's first cabinet in 1870 he had pushed through a process of reform and modernisation, often in the face of bitter opposition from the military establishment, and the result was a gradual change in the composition and outlook of the Army. Flogging in peacetime was abolished immediately (it was retained as a punishment in the field, and was used during the Zulu War), easing one of the more brutalising factors in the Other Ranks' lot. Two years later, active service was shortened from twelve years with the Colours to six with the Colours and six on reserve. This was intended both to attract a better quality of recruit—and standards of literacy in the

Melvill's Ride To Glory, a modern reconstruction by American artist Bud Bradshaw, showing Lieutenant and Adjutant Teignmouth Melvill, 1/24th, attempting to save the Queen's Colour of his battalion at Isandlwana. Melvill is shown wearing the undress frock and carrying the Colour in its leather case. Lt. N. J. A. Coghill, 1/24th, who came to Melvill's aid, was wearing a blue patrol jacket, and probably riding breeches. Both officers were killed in the action. (By kind permission of the artist)

lower ranks did increase markedly over the decade—and to provide a large pool of well-trained reservists who were still young.

The move attracted considerable criticism on the grounds that it replaced toughened veterans in the ranks with inexperienced youngsters, and it is interesting to note that experience in the Zulu War tends to bear this out. Many observers were struck by the youth of the short-service men, particularly those sent out after Isandlwana, who seemed to have been rather too impressed by the Zulus' fearsome reputation, and who remained prone to false alarms, particularly at night. Such alarms were not only wearing on the nerves; they could be dangerous, and on more than one occasion night piquets were mistaken for the enemy, and shot.

There was a change, too, amongst the officer class. The system by which officers had purchased their commissions, leading to a hierarchy based on personal fortune rather than competence or experience, was abolished in 1871. Many senior officers still held commands acquired under the old system, and the necessity of a private income meant that they remained a social élite, but there was an increasing emphasis on proficiency and training among junior officers. New, more fluid tactical theories were beginning to replace the rigid columns and lines of the Napoleonic era, which in turn encouraged greater self-reliance and flexibility. Such theories were largely intended for the European theatre, but in fact the British Army found itself employed in the role of Imperial policeman, where no two opponents or circumstances were exactly alike. Although over-confidence and inexperience often resulted in defeats early in such campaigns, the Army learned the hard way how to adapt to particular conditions.

Another of Cardwell's reforms, in 1873, was to link infantry battalions in pairs and tie them to a specific district within the United Kingdom where their recruitment and training was to be based. The 109 Line Infantry Regiments were identified by numbers, but many also had a subsidiary title reflecting their regional links. The 3rd Regiment, historically known as 'the Buffs' because of the colour of their facings, were the East Kents; the 24th Regiment were the 2nd Warwickshires, and so on. The first 25 regiments were each composed of two battalions, the remainder of one. In 1881 this process would be taken to its logical conclusion and several of the single-battalion regiments were amalgamated to form a single regiment; e.g. the 88th Regiment, the Connaught Rangers, were joined with the 94th to form the 1st and 2nd Battalions of the Connaught Rangers. In theory, one battalion was always supposed to be stationed at the depot whilst the other served overseas, but in fact the demands of Empire meant that significantly more were overseas at any given time.

It was most unusual for battalions of the same regiment to be serving together, though the 24th achieved this distinction, and it is interesting to note the effects of Cardwell's reforms upon them. The 1/24th had been sent overseas in 1867, and had arrived at the Cape from Gibraltar in 1875. Most of its men had enlisted under the old long-service system and, although nearly half of them were replaced by drafts from home before the start of the Zulu War, as many as 80% of its NCOs

OR's glengarry badge, 24th Regt. (above), and officers' belt clasp. (Collection of Keith Reeves)

course, but its composition was markedly different. It arrived in South Africa in March 1878, and was employed 'mopping up' on the Frontier. The soldiers were mostly short-service men whose youth struck observers in marked contrast to their sister battalion, and they included a much higher proportion of men with Welsh accents, bearing witness to the success of recruiting drives around the depot in Brecon. They, too, however, soon learned their craft amongst the kloofs and bush of the Frontier, which gave them a considerable advantage over their counterparts later in the war who had no experience to offset against their opponents' reputation.

Organisationally, each battalion consisted ideally—according to *Regulations for Field Forces, South Africa 1878*—of 30 officers and 866 men, though few were ever up to strength because of casualties, sickness and so on; on the eve of campaign the 1/24th, for example, had less than 700 men available for duty. Each battalion included a band—who were employed as stretcher-bearers in action—and was divided up into eight lettered companies, each ideally consisting of 107

Two splendid portraits of colour-sergeants wearing the dress tunic. Above is Col. Sgt. Anthony Booth, 80th Regt., who won the VC for his part in the action at Ntombe Drift in March 1879; right is Col. Sgt. Smith, 90th LI, who won the DCM during the Ninth Cape Frontier War. Note that Light Infantry wear the chevrons on both sleeves. Smith is also wearing the home service Light Infantry shako, and has a 'marksman' badge above his left cuff. Although the 90th wore their facing colours on the tunic collar and cuffs, there was no facing panel on the cuff of the frock. As well as being excellent uniform references, these portraits suggest something of the character of such men. (Royal Collection)

remained, and company photographs show a large number of men with Long Service and Good Conduct stripes. The men were perfectly acclimatised, and well used to serving under their officers and NCOs. They had fought throughout the Ninth Cape Frontier War, including the battle of Centane in February 1878, where their concentrated volley fire had broken a massed Xhosa attack. Gen. Cunynghame had been most impressed: 'there was no duty whatever to which the 24th Regiment could not be found equal to'.

The 2/24th would earn its own eulogies in due

The OR's 1877-81 pattern tunic, showing the collar patches, cuff panels, trefoil braid, piping, collar badge and shoulder numeral. This particular tunic was worn by the 7th Royal Fusiliers who did not serve in Zululand, though the pattern is the same as for those who did. The practice of wearing Long Service and Good Conduct chevrons on the right sleeve was switched to the left shortly after the Zulu War. (National Army Museum)

Other Ranks and three officers—a captain, a lieutenant and a second lieutenant. The remaining officer establishment consisted of a lieutenant-colonel (in command), two majors, an adjutant, a paymaster and a quartermaster.

Infantry Uniforms

Although there had been experiments with dull and neutral-coloured clothing in the 1850s, khaki remained in service in India only, and the troops in Zululand went into action in a variety of traditional scarlets, blues and greens. There were concessions to practicality, however, in that both officers and ORs had a choice of jackets, for smarter occasions or for when duties required a practical working dress.

Officers

The officers' tunic, with its regimental facing colours on the collar and cuffs and its ornate gold braid, appears only in formal photographs and was not worn in the field. Instead, officers wore either a blue patrol jacket or a scarlet frock, the latter being sometimes known as the Scarlet Patrol, or the India-Pattern Frock, reflecting its origins.

The patrol jacket was of dark blue cloth, edged all round by flat, black 1in. mohair braid. It was decorated across the front with four rows of black ¼in. flat mohair plait; each double row had an eye loop in the centre (above and below) and ended in a double drop-loop. The jacket fastened down the front with hooks and eyes, but there were four netted olivets on the right side which fastened through the braid loops on the left. The cuffs were ornamented with Austrian knots in the same braid, and the back seams each had a double row of braid ending at each end in a crow's foot design, and with double eyes in the centre. Prior to 1881 the patrol jacket had no shoulder straps.

The undress frock was made of light cloth or serge, and was fastened by five regimental buttons down the front. The cuffs and shoulder straps were also scarlet, but the collar was completely in the regimental facing colour. The facing colours for

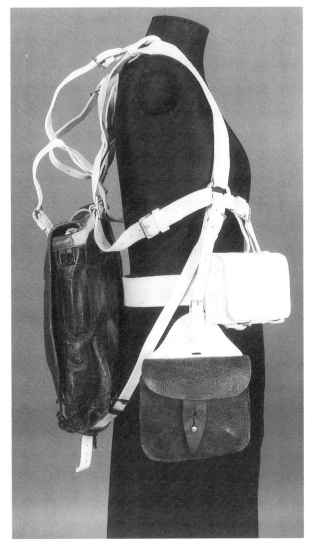
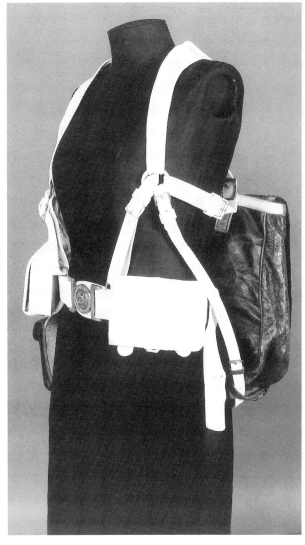

the regiments who fought in Zululand were as follows: 2/3rd buff, 2/4th blue, 1/13th blue, 2/21st blue, 1st and 2nd/24th green, 57th yellow, 58th black, 80th yellow, 88th green, 90th buff, 94th Lincoln green, and 99th yellow (the 3/60th Rifles and 91st Highlanders wore distinctive uniforms described below). The frock was piped down the front, up the back skirt vents, and round the shoulder straps in white. The shoulder straps also bore the regimental number, embroidered in gold. Rank was indicated by gold braid on the cuff and by collar badges. A single line of braid around the cuff, with an Austrian knot above and below the cuff, was worn by lieutenants and second lieutenants. Captains wore a double row of braid, with the same knots above and below. Majors also had a double row, but with a second line of looped 'bullet hole' braid above the upper row. Lieutenant-colonels and above had a similar looped row below the second row.

The universal rank system signified rank by a series of badges on either side of the collar opening. A gold embroidered crown indicated lieutenant-colonel, a star major, and a crown and star captain. In theory a crown on its own indicated a lieutenant, and a star on its own a second lieutenant, but in practice neither of these ranks wore badges on the frock. In some regiments—certainly the 4th and 24th—junior officers wore regimental badges in place of rank ones. On the blue patrol jackets, only lieutenant-colonels and above seem to have worn collar rank badges. On the full dress tunic the badges were silver.

In practice, there was considerable variation in

The Valise pattern equipment. The exact design of these buff waist pouches post-dates the Zulu War, but in all other respects it is correct for 1879. The two looped straps at the back retained the rolled greatcoat, with the mess tin strap below. The valise itself was not usually worn on the march in Zululand, but carried on the regimental transport. The black expense pouch was often worn at the back in its place. (National Army Museum)

the field) that the 2/24th preferred OR's frocks stripped of all decoration except the collar facing-tab.

Officers' headgear varied between the dark blue glengarry side-cap with black ribbons and red tourie, worn with a regimental badge on the left; a dark blue peaked forage cap; and the foreign service helmet. The forage cap had a square black leather peak, and a wide band of black oak-leaf pattern lace all round, with a black cord button and design on the top. It was worn with the regimental badge over the numeral on the front.

The foreign service helmet was white with a brass spike and chin-chain, though on campaign these were replaced with a white 'cap' and leather strap repectively. The regimental badge was authorised for wear on the front. In 1878 a new star plate, with the regimental number in front and surmounted by a crown, had been approved, but, with the possible exception of a few senior officers, it does not seem to have been issued to the troops before the start of the Zulu campaign. Instead the old 1869-78 shako plate was retained; this consisted of a laurel wreath surmounted by a crown, with the numeral cut out in the centre. In practice, the combination of white helmet and brass plate proved the most conspicuous part of the soldiers' uniform, an obvious and tempting target, and all ranks used to remove the plate and dull down the helmet with improvised dyes ranging from tea, coffee, and boiled mimosa bark to cow-dung. Again, there was considerable variation between regiments regarding the wearing of helmet plates. In some it was the fashion for officers alone to retain them. A number of plates have been recovered from the battlefield of Isandlwana, but very few, bearing no relationship with the number of casualties, and making any conclusion about their distribution impossible.

the design of frocks, often within the same regiment. A photograph of officers of the 90th during the campaign shows both piped and unpiped frocks, and several have breast pockets. Certain styles obviously followed a regimental fashion. Officers of the 80th Regiment appear to have worn unpiped frocks, with the shoulder straps replaced by leather pads. It was quite common for officers to wear the OR's frock; and there is a tantalising suggestion (supported by a surviving example and by analysis of photographs of Lt. G. Bromhead in

Officers' trousers were dark blue with a thin red stripe down the outer seam. For mounted duties it was common to wear buff Bedford cord riding breeches. Boots were of black leather, although, again, there was considerable variation, brown leather riding boots and leggings or leather or canvas being common.

Officers' weapons consisted of the 1822 pattern Infantry Officers' Sword, with a steel scabbard, carried suspended by two slings from a white leather sword-belt, fastened with a gilt Regimental clasp. A number of privately purchased revolvers were carried, of which the 1872 pattern Adams was the most popular. The Sam Browne belt, which was becoming increasingly popular within the British Army, does not seem to have been worn in Zululand. Instead, officers carried their revolvers in a brown leather holster either on a strap over the shoulder, or attached to a waist belt. Waist belts usually had a snake-hook fastener, and small ammunition pouches were commonly worn on them. Field glasses were also carried in leather cases.

Other ranks

The Other Ranks' tunic was scarlet, and fastened down the front by seven brass general service buttons (bearing the royal arms). The facing colours were displayed on a pointed tab on either side of the collar, and on a pointed cuff panel. The cuffs were edged in white tape forming a trefoil knot above the point. The tunic was piped round the bottom edge of the collar, down the front, and up the back vents of the skirt. The shoulder straps were also piped, and bore the regimental numeral in either brass or white metal. A Regimental badge was worn on the collar tabs. The badges for those Regiments which fought in Zululand were: 2/3rd, the Dragon of Cadwalladar; 2/4th, the Lion of England; 1/13th, a bugle and strings surmounted by a crown; 2/21st, a grenade with a thistle on the ball; 1st and 2/24th, a sphinx; 57th, a laurel wreath and scroll bearing the honour 'Albuhera'; 58th, the Castle and Key of Gibraltar; 80th, the Staffordshire knot; 88th, a crowned harp; 90th, a stringed bugle; 94th, an elephant; 99th, the Duke of Edinburgh's cypher, two 'A's on either side of a coronet.

In Line Infantry regiments rank chevrons were worn on the right sleeve only, but Fusiliers, Rifles, Highlanders and Light Infantry wore them on both sleeves. The distinctions were as follows: one white worsted chevron, lance corporal; two white chevrons, corporal; three white chevrons, lance sergeant; three gold lace chevrons, sergeant; three gold chevrons surmounted by a crown, staff sergeant; three gold chevrons surmounted by a cross Union Flag device, colour sergeant; four gold chevrons surmounted by a crown, worn above the cuff, sergeant major. Long Service and Good Conduct stripes were awarded to qualifying privates and lance corporals, to a maximum of seven badges, for 2, 5, 12, 16, 18, 21 and 26 years' service. The badge itself was a white chevron point uppermost, worn above the right cuff. Various trade and proficiency badges were also worn.

The OR's frock was of similar design, but had only five buttons, and was not piped down the front. In theory both the collar tabs and cuff facings should have been retained, but this varied from regiment to regiment, some preferring to leave off the cuff facing. The 3rd, 21st and 90th had plain red cuffs (but retaining the white tape

OR's buff leather waist belt and ammunition pouch, 24th Regiment, of the type worn in Zululand. (National Army Museum)

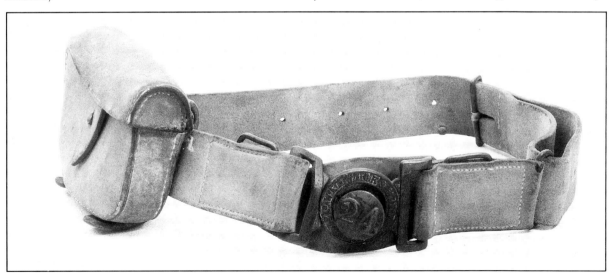

trefoil), though the 24th seem to have retained the facing colour.

Both the tunic and frock appear in photographs of the Zulu War. Whilst it is possible that the tunic was only worn for the photographer, it seems likely both were worn in the field even within the same regiment, though the frock was undoubtedly the more common as it was more practical.

OR's headgear consisted of the glengarry cap, with regimental badge; and the foreign service helmet, usually denuded of its fittings, and dyed, as described for the officers. OR's trousers were dark blue with a red stripe down the outer seam. Boots were black, and worn in marching order with black leather leggings, which were fastened down the outside by a series of loops passing through one another, and fixed at the top by a strap.

Infantry equipment was the 1871 Valise Pattern. This consisted of a buff leather waist belt, fastened by a regimental clasp. On either side of it were two buff ammunition pouches carrying 20 rounds apiece. Carried on a leather sling over the left shoulder was the Oliver pattern water-bottle, a small coopered D-section barrel with a screw stopper. A white haversack was worn over the left shoulder. In full marching order a waterproofed black canvas valise was designed to be carried at the small of the back, supported by braces attached to the waist belt. A rolled grey greatcoat was carried across the shoulders, with a mess-tin below, usually in a black container; the glengarry was usually tucked under the straps on the outside of the greatcoat. A black leather 'expense' pouch containing a further 30 rounds of ammunition was carried below the right-hand buff pouch. In practice, the troops in Zululand do not seem to have worn their valises, which were usually carried on the regimental transport instead. The expense pouch was often therefore carried in place of the valise, at the back of the belt. It also seems fairly common for the greatcoat to have been carried *en banderole*.

Two of the battalions which fought in Zululand were Light Infantry—the 1/13th and 90th—but their uniforms were the same as Line regiments' except in the areas discussed. They also had green glengarries rather than the Line's blue. The 90th were also nominally a Scottish Regiment (Perthshire Volunteers), but this was not reflected in

Unidentified private. 4th Regiment, 1879. He is wearing the undress frock, with a LS & GC stripe on the right cuff and a marksman badge on the other. The collar badge is the Lion of England. The helmet spike and chin-chain were not worn on active service. (Keith Reeves Collection)

their uniform in any way, except the title 'Perthshire' on their badge.

Scottish uniforms

Three of the other battalions—the 2/21st, 91st and 99th—also had Scottish associations. The 2/21st (Royal Scots Fusiliers) wore the same as Line Infantry with a number of minor differences. Both glengarries and officers' forage caps had a distinctive diced band of red, white and green (the last where the two lines of red crossed). Officers' frocks were similar to their Line equivalents, but instead of shoulder straps had twisted crimson cords, and the regiment's grenade badge was also worn on the collar in place of rank badges. Officers, but apparently not Other Ranks, also seem to have retained the grenade helmet plate.

The battalion also maintained pipers, who feature in at least one contemporary engraving showing troops on the march in Zululand. They wore the usual helmet, but with a Scottish jacket with rounded skirt front and gauntlet cuffs, and the kilt. The jacket was dark blue, and fastened by white metal diamond-shaped buttons. There were three buttons on each cuff, and three on each shaped pocket flap on the front skirts. The jacket was piped red around the bottom of the collar, around the cuffs, and in line with each of the buttons on the cuffs and skirts. A white metal grenade badge was worn either side of the collar opening. The kilt was of Royal Stewart Tartan, with a red rosette on the right side of the kilt. The hose were red with a blue diamond pattern, and the sporran was white with black tassels. A black leather waist belt with a white metal plate bearing the regimental device was worn, as were the ordinary haversack and water-bottle. The pipe-bag and ribbons were also of Royal Stewart Tartan. Alas, though the 21st played a significant part at Ulundi, there is no evidence to suggest that the pipes were played during the battle.

The 91st (Princess Louise's Argyllshire) Highlanders did wear a characteristic Highland uniform, although this regiment wore trews rather than the kilt. Contemporary photographs show officers wearing both the dress doublet and the frock in the field. The doublet had gauntlet cuffs and shaped Inverness skirt-flaps. It was scarlet with yellow cuffs and collar, and fastened by eight regimental buttons down the front. There was a band of gold lace around the top of the collar and around the cuffs, with three loops of gold braid and three buttons on each cuff and skirt-flap. The shoulder cords were also of twisted gold braid. There was white piping around the bottom of the collar, down the front, and in a double row round the Inverness skirt-flaps. Rank distinctions were worn on the collar by all ranks; and there were further distinctions indicated by the cuff braid, colonels having four extra narrow bands of braid, majors three, captains two, and lieutenants one. The frock was also scarlet, but with only five buttons down the front, and the facing colour on the collar only. The Inverness skirts were omitted, and instead the skirts were rounded at the front with a pocket flap on either side. Cuffs were again of the gauntlet style, with three buttons, and there were also three buttons on the skirt pockets. The bottom edge of the collar, down the front and around the skirts, pocket flaps, shoulder straps and lines to cuff and pocket buttons were piped with narrow gold braid. The cuffs were edged with a slightly wider gold braid.

Even within the same photograph, there is considerable variation in the style of frocks evident. One officer has six buttons rather than five, while another has diamond-shaped buttons rather than round. Of two officers wearing the doublet,

The Oliver pattern water-bottle. (Author's Collection)

one has a breast pocket, the other does not. Headgear is the ubiquitous helmet, mostly without decoration, though one officer appears to be wearing a puggaree of animal skin, and another has an object attached on one side which appears to be a small plume or animal tail. The helmets generally appear to have been stained, and the bands around them appear very dark. Most of the officers are wearing the usual paraphernalia of straps and haversacks, as well as the undress sword belt, which was white with a regimental clasp. Swords are the 1865 pattern Scottish broadsword with a crossguard rather than the basket hilt, carried in a steel scabbard. Trousers were of the Campbell of Cawdor tartan, and tucked into knee-boots, which may well have been 'veld boots' of local manufacture—these were of brown leather, and laced part of the way up the front, with a strap at the top on the outside.

ORs of the 91st wore the undress frock, which was scarlet with a yellow collar, rounded skirts with pocket flaps, and gauntlet cuffs. The piping around the base of the collar, cuffs and in line with the cuff and skirt buttons was white. The regimental badge—a boar's head—was worn on the collar, and the numerals '91' in brass on the shoulder straps. Trews were as for officers, and leggings, boots and all other equipment were as for Line Infantry. A photograph of the battalion lined up in Zululand, however, shows that, with the exception of one man who has buff ammunition pouches, all the others have black pouches of a slightly older design.

Like the 21st, the 99th (Duke of Edinburgh's) Regiment had little about their uniform to suggest their Scottish connections, apart from a diced band (red, white and yellow) on the glengarry and officers' forage cap. However, despite the fact that the regiment sailed straight from Chatham in November 1878 in response to Chelmsford's request for reinforcements on the eve of the campaign, a photograph of them at the Lower Drift early in the war indicates that they were still wearing outdated items no longer common to the other regiments. In particular, they are wearing an 1872 pattern undress frock; this lacked the collar patches and cuff trefoil of the later pattern. Instead, the whole collar was the facing colour (yellow for the 99th), and the cuffs were plain, with

White foreign service helmet (the top vent on this example has sunk slightly with age), bearing the shako plate of the 57th (West Middlesex) Regiment. (Keith Reeves Collection)

a single loop of white braid. The bottom edge of the collar and the shoulder straps were edged white, and the regimental numerals and collar badges were worn as normal. The equipment is Valise pattern, but with the black ammunition pouches described earlier. In the photograph the helmets appear clean and the shako plate is clearly visible, although at this point the battalion had not been in the Colony long, and may well have followed the usual practice of removing the plate and dying the helmet and equipment straps later. Unfortunately no evidence has come to light of the uniform worn by officers in the field, but there is no reason to suppose it would have been different from that of Line Infantry.

The Rifles

The 3/60th were the only Rifle battalion to take part in the campaign, arriving in March 1879 and taking part in the Eshowe relief expedition and the advance of the 1st Division. Their uniform was extremely distinctive. Officially it consisted of very

A company of the 99th Regiment crossing the Thukela at the Lower Drift. The single loop of cuff braid identifying the pattern of frock worn by this regiment can clearly be seen, right. Note that the men retain their helmet plates. (Local History Museum, Durban)

dark 'rifle green' jacket and trousers; however, due to problems with finding a suitable dye which did not fade, the true colour was very close to black. Officers wore an undress frock, fastened with four black buttons. There were no shoulder straps, and the collar was red, but this was largely obscured by two wide bands of black braid around the top and bottom. Trousers were of the same colour, with black boots and leggings. Field officers wore black riding breeches reinforced on the inside with black dyed buckskin, and black boots with steel spurs. The helmet was the standard foreign service type, dyed brown, but unlike most other regiments the 60th did not remove their helmet plates. These were an inconspicuous black metal Maltese cross, with a bugle centre device, on a red field. Officers' equipment consisted of black leather waist belts, fastened with a snake hook or square buckle—both painted black—and with a black leather revolver holster, and a sword with a steel hilt and black leather knot in a black scabbard. Any other equipment—field glasses, water-bottle etc—would have been predominantly black.

The uniform of the ORs was similarly sombre. They wore the same helmet, and a dark frock fastened by five black bakelite buttons. The bottom edge of the collar was piped red, and there was a loop of braid on the cuffs. The battalion number was embroidered in scarlet on the shoulder strap. Rank chevrons, worn on both sleeves for Rifle regiments, were black on a red background. Trousers were black with no stripe. Leggings and boots were black, and the equipment was the Valise pattern but with all straps black and all buckles of brass. The waist belt was fastened by a snake-hook rather than the usual locket. The haversack, worn over the right shoulder, was black, as were the water-bottle straps. The greatcoat, however, was the more usual grey. All Other Ranks were armed with the sword-bayonet, and the slings on the rifle were black leather.

Infantry Colours

Each infantry battalion carried two Colours, the Queen's Colour and the Regimental Colour. The Colours were six feet flying by five feet six inches deep, and had fringes, cords and tassels of mixed gold and crimson. The pike was topped either by a brass or gilt device of a lion surmounting a crown, or a less complex spearhead. The Queen's Colour was basically the national standard, the Great Union Flag, and bore a gold embroidered Imperial crown in the centre above the regimental numeral. Thus the famous Queen's Colour of the 1/24th, which Lts. Melvill and Coghill tried to save at Isandlwana, was the Union flag with a crown above the numeral XXIV. The 2/24th's Queen's Colour was similar but with a scroll beneath the numeral bearing the title II Battalion. The Regimental Colour was unique to each battalion. It was of the regimental facing colour, with a small Union flag in the dexter canton (the top corner abutting the pike), and a regimental device and battle honours. For example, the Queen's Colour of the 58th (Rutlandshire) Regiment was the Union with a crown above the numeral LVIII; but the Regimental Colour was black with the Cross of St George, the Union in the dexter canton, a red and gold LVIII in the centre, surrounded by RUTLANDSHIRE with the Union wreath around, a crown above, and the motto MONTIS INSIGNIA CALPE below. In 1879 it had ten battle honours on scrolls on either side of the central device. The Buffs carried their Colours into action at Nyezane, and several battalions carried them at Ulundi, including the 58th, who achieved the distinction, at Laing's Nek two years later in the Transvaal War, of being the last infantry regiment to carry their Colours into action. When not in action, the Colours were furled and protected by a heavy leather case with a brass top.

Appearance in the field

It is interesting to note that there seems to have been no provision for replacing worn out or damaged clothing during the campaign. Zululand's climate can be one of extremes, and this was certainly the case in 1879, when baking days alternated with sudden chilling downpours during the summer months, and a biting frost was common on winter nights. Much of the country is covered in thornbush, and the rigours of life in the open took a heavy toll on soldiers' uniforms.

Infantry Colours. The Regimental Colour of the 94th, left, and Queen's Colour of the 21st Royal Scots Fusiliers. Although this photograph was taken in 1881 during the Transvaal War, where these Colours had an interesting history, the same Colours were also carried in Zululand. (National Army Museum)

Of the 1/13th one observer wrote: 'their uniforms were in rags, and patched with different colours, some had no boots . . . their helmets . . . were covered in old shirts . . . and their belts and rifles dirtied to order'. The regimental history of the 2/21st states: 'Each man endeavoured as best he could to repair the rents and holes in his apparel; but the material obtainable was most unsuitable, being neither the colour nor texture of the material itself. Patches of biscuit bags, blankets, waterproof sheets, may cover deficiencies, but they do not add to the splendours of a soldier's uniform!'

There is no reason to suppose that the experience of these two regiments was in any way unique. Sketches by Lt. W. W. Lloyd of the 24th show men of his regiment in patched uniforms, with battered helmets or civilian hats; and Pte. Gissop of the 17th Lancers wondered 'what people would have thought could they only have seen us with our clothes torn and patched, belts and saddles dirty, bits rusty, boots without blacking or grease, and so lamentable in appearance from the Regiment which left England so clean and smart such a short time ago'. Photographs on campaign show both officers and men wearing civilian hats instead of helmets—clearly this was as much a matter of necessity as of choice.

A night piquet of the 94th Regiment, Upoko River, Zululand. The men are wearing their equipment buckled over the greatcoats. (Author's Collection)

Weapons

The standard infantry weapon was the 1875 Mark II pattern Martini-Henry rifle, the earlier version of which had begun to replace the Snider from 1871. It was a single shot breech-loader with a simple mechanism, activated by lowering a lever behind the trigger guard. This caused the breech-block to drop, allowing the cartridge to be inserted into the chamber at the top of the breech. The cartridge was a .45in. Boxer type, with a hardened but unjacketed lead bullet of 480 grains. The barrel had seven grooves and the bullet emerged with a muzzle velocity of 1,350 feet per second. It was sighted up to 1,000 yards, but its effective battlefield range was half that, and it was particularly deadly at 350 yards. By the time of the Zulu War it was in service around the world, and had proved itself on the Eastern Cape at Nyumaxa in January 1878. Sir Arthur Cunynghame had been impressed: 'At no time had the power of the Martini-Henry rifle been more conspicuously shown; indeed, it was perhaps the first occasion when it had been fairly used by the British army.' It was considered to possess the necessary stopping-power to lay out a charging warrior in his tracks, and the heavy bullet certainly inflicted the ghastly wounds associated with its type—small entry holes with horrific exit wounds.

It was not without its faults, however. With frequent use the barrel became hot and fouled, exaggerating the already pronounced recoil. The

The 91st Highlanders on the march in Zululand. Note the pipers, centre left, and the fact that blankets are worn 'en banderole'. (National Army Museum)

extractor grip might tear through the soft brass of the cartridge, causing it to jam; and since the forestock did not encircle the barrel over-heating could mean burnt fingers on the left hand. To counter this veterans of the Cape Frontier War sewed bullock hide around the forestock.

The Martini-Henry weighed 9lb., was 4ft 1½ins. long, and had a buff leather sling. ORs below the rank of sergeant carried a triangular socket bayonet 21½ins. long, which gave a combined reach of over six feet; the bayonet was nicknamed 'the lunger' as a result. It was carried in a black leather scabbard with brass fittings on the left rear of the waist belt. Sergeants and above carried the 1871 pattern sword bayonet, which had a steel hilt with a chequered leather grip, and a blade with a double curve; it was carried in a black scabbard with steel fittings.

In view of the controversy surrounding the question of the supply of ammunition at Isandlwana, it is worth considering the design of the boxes used to contain the battalion supplies. As early as 1874 the *Treatise on Ammunition* provided plans of the Small Arms Ammunition Box, Mark IV, which was capable of carrying 560 Snider rounds or 600 Martini-Henry rounds. This was modified slightly by the Mark V and VI models of 1875. In each case, the boxes were made of teak or mahogany, and lined with tin to protect the contents on overseas service. Each pattern was encircled by two copper retaining bands, screwed into place; but it was *not* necessary to remove the bands in order to gain access to the ammunition. Access was via a grooved sliding panel in the lid; this was held in place by one screw, but it was generally recognised that in times of emergency a sharp blow, or even a kick, to the outer edge would snap the screw and dislodge the panel. The tin liner could be pulled back by means of a handle situated at the panel opening. It is not clear which pattern of boxes were in use at Isandlwana—Mark IV, V or VI—but in each case the quartermasters would have known better than to waste time unscrewing the retaining bands.

Logistics

Before leaving the infantry, it is worth considering the logistical back-up necessary to maintain a battalion in the field. Each battalion had to carry its own ammunition, tents (the eight-man Bell tent—after the man who invented it, rather than its shape), entrenching tools and medical equipment, not to mention rations. In Zululand these usually consisted of 'mealies' (local corn carried in 200lb. bags), tough army biscuit in heavy wooden boxes, and tinned 'bully beef'. Fresh meat was usually 'on the hoof' and vegetables were procured where available. Wood's column included a field bakery. These requirements alone could take up 17 wagons, without the luxury of the officers' personal baggage, and the men's bottled beer. If there was no fuel around, that too would have to be transported. For cavalry regiments, whose British-bred horses would not eat coarse local grasses, fodder, too, would have to be carried.

There were a limited number of Army General Service wagons available, but they were not ideal, since their narrow carriage, intended for European roads, made them unstable in southern Africa. The solution was to purchase local transport, which Chelmsford's harassed and inexperienced transport staff did, often at inflated prices. The wagons themselves were large and heavy, sometimes tented, often with a half-tent covering the rear portion only. They required between 16 and 18 oxen apiece to pull them; and if the oxen were to remain healthy they needed 16 hours each day for rest and grazing, which reduced their travelling potential to about ten miles per day. On trackless country, roads seamed by dongas or turned into a quagmire by sudden rain, it was much less.

Shortage of transport remained a major headache throughout the war, and it is impossible to ignore the extent to which it dominated Chelmsford's strategy. The camp at Isandlwana was unlaagered because the wagons were about to return to Rorke's Drift to fetch supplies; Rorke's Drift proved so defensible simply because those same supplies were available to build barricades. The Second Invasion moved at such a methodical pace so that forts could be erected to guard the staging posts as the convoys slogged back and forth along the lines of communication. Even in battle the wagons formed the surest means of defence, the *laager*. This was based on the Boer practice of circling wagons for protection in hostile country at the end of a day's trek. In 1879, especially after Isandlwana, transport wagons were drawn into one or more linked square laager, which was often entrenched. The usual method was to dig a trench several paces beyond the wagon line, piling the earth up inside to form a parapet. The troops would then sleep between the parapet and the wagons at night, and man the parapet at times of alarm. The wagon-drivers themselves were usually civilian contractors, with African *Voorloopers*, who walked at the head of the train, controlling the oxen with long whips.

Another Transvaal War photo, this time of the 3/60th Rifles at Mount Prospect Camp. The uniform is the same as worn in Zululand; the single loop of braid on the cuffs is clearly visible, as are NCOs' chevrons. Most of the helmets here have both the Maltese Cross badge and the spike. The 1879 medal ribbon is just visible on most of the jackets. (Royal Greenjackets Museum, Winchester)

Cavalry

At the beginning of the campaign Chelmsford had no regular cavalry regiments at his disposal—something of a drawback given the cavalry's traditional roles of scouting and pursuit. He did, however, have two understrength squadrons of Mounted Infantry, who were distributed throughout the invading columns. The MI consisted of selected soldiers from infantry regiments mounted on locally acquired horses. They wore the foreign service helmet, with no fittings, and the undress frock of their battalions, with buff Bedford cord riding breeches, leggings and boots. Instead of infantry equipment they carried loop-style ammunition bandoliers over the left shoulder. Waist belts, water-bottles and haversacks may have been worn on occasions. Officers wore cord riding breeches, boots, and patrol jackets or frocks from their own battalions. Despite the mixed origins of this force it performed extremely well, and paved the way for greater reliance on Mounted Infantry units in later campaigns.

When news of the Isandlwana débâcle reached London, two full regiments were embarked for South Africa: the 1st (King's) Dragoon Guards, and the 17th (Duke of Cambridge's Own) Lancers. Both created a mixed reaction when they arrived in Natal. The settlers were impressed that such dashing regiments had been sent to their aid, but sceptical about the value of British-bred horses. The heavy cavalry mounts had indeed suffered badly on the long voyage out, and once ashore refused to eat the local grasses. The regiments were therefore allowed to make their way up country slowly to allow the horses time to recover; they did not reach the front until May. Here they were brigaded together to form the Cavalry Brigade under Maj.-Gen. Marshall, and attached to the 2nd Division. Both emerged from the campaign with distinction; the 17th, with one squadron of Dragoons, charged from the square at Ulundi to turn the Zulu retreat into a rout, and it was a patrol of the Dragoons who finally captured King Cetshwayo.

Each cavalry regiment consisted of four squadrons, each of 120 privates, 22 NCOs (including four artificers and two trumpeters), and six officers; and a headquarters staff, to a nominal total of 653 men. The Dragoon Guards were almost up to strength with 649, the 17th slightly under with 622.

Lancer officers' uniform

In neither regiment did the Dress Regulations make many concessions to the practicalities of service in the field beyond replacing home service headgear with the inevitable helmet. The officers of the 17th Lancers wore their full dress 1876 pattern tunic. This was dark blue with a white plastron front, white collar and cuffs, and white piping along the leading edge of the skirt, around the bottom, and along the back and arm seams. It was double-breasted, with two rows of gilt buttons bearing the regimental death's head device, the rows being eight inches apart at the top and four inches at the waist; the last two buttons were flattened to fit under the waist girdle. There were two more buttons at the back above the slashed skirt panels, which bore three more buttons, and were edged all round with gold cord. A small button on each shoulder secured a loop of gold braid. There was a one-inch band of gold lace around the top of the collar and around the pointed cuffs. Field officers had a double row of

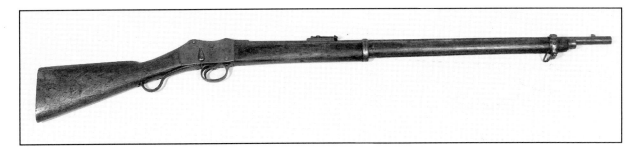

The .45 Martini-Henry Rifle, Mark 2; the standard infantry arm during the Zulu War. (National Army Museum)

gold around the cuffs and a narrow band around the bottom of the collar. Rank badges (in silver) were worn on the collar by all officers. Trousers were dark blue with a double white stripe with a blue line between.

Dress Regulations called for officers to wear a gold waist girdle with two crimson stripes, but this was not worn in Zululand. There were other unofficial practical modifications, too. It is hard to imagine anything more conspicuous in the bright African sun than a glaring white helmet and plastron. When photographed in Natal the Lancers' helmets were still pristine, but by the time they were in Zululand they had achieved the same muddied look as those of the infantry, and no doubt by the same means. The plastron was obscured simply by buttoning it over to reveal the less conspicuous blue reverse side.

The officers' dress pouch belt does seem to have been retained in action, however. This was gold, with a white centre line; the plate, chain, pickers, buckle tip and slide were all of silver. The pouch itself was blue leather with a silver top engraved round the edge and with an entwined 'VR' cypher in gilt. Individual portraits suggest that it was fashionable within the regiment to wear the belt with the plate high in the centre of the chest and the top mount under the shoulder cords. The dress sword belt, carrying the 1822 Light Cavalry sabre in a steel scabbard, was gold with a white centre line and a snake clasp, the slings being the same but with gilt buckles. It was officially supposed to be worn under the tunic, though photographs in Zululand show several officers wearing it outside. Indeed, many seem to have preferred unofficial

The Mark V Small Arms Ammunition box, showing the copper retaining straps. Access to the ammunition was via a sliding centre panel, missing on this example. For overseas garrisons the box was lined with tinfoil. (Royal Regiment of Wales, Brecon)

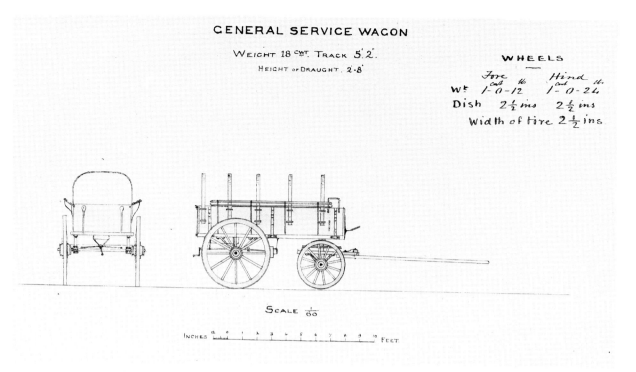

The General Service wagon, the standard transport wagon of the British Army. From a series of sketches depicting transport vehicles during the Zulu War. (National Army Museum)

brown leather belts with revolver holsters. Some also discarded their trousers in favour of the popular cord riding breeches.

Lancer OR's uniform
The OR's tunic was of similar pattern to the officers': blue, with a white plastron front, white collar, pointed cuffs, and white piping down the leading edge of the skirt, round the bottom, along the back seams and around the back skirt flaps. The buttons were of brass and regimental pattern. The shoulder cords were single loops of yellow braid. NCOs' chevrons were gold, worn on the right sleeve only, and Long Service and Good Conduct stripes were yellow, and worn above the right cuff. Trousers were dark blue with a double white stripe. The official waist girdle was yellow worsted with two red stripes, but it was not worn on campaign, and nor were the yellow body lines. Like the officers, the ORs reversed their plastrons to show the blue side.

A white canvas haversack was worn over the right shoulder, and a white pouch belt, with brass fittings and black leather pouch, was worn over the left shoulder, as was the Oliver pattern waterbottle. The sword belt was of white leather with a brass snake-hook fastener. The 1864 Cavalry Trooper's Sword was carried in a steel scabbard.

Photographs of the regiment on campaign show buff ammunition pouches worn on either side of the waist belt buckle, since in addition to the lance the men carried Martini-Henry carbines. The main weapon, the lance, was the 1868 pattern—nine feet long, and made of 'male' bamboo, which has less pith and is therefore stronger than the more common 'female' bamboo. The blade was of cast steel, as was the shoe. A red-over-white pennon was fixed to the wood just below the blade, and there was a white rawhide grip at the point of balance.

There is very little evidence concerning horse furniture, but both Lancers and Dragoons were issued some of the new 1878 pattern 'Angle Iron Arch' saddles, though they were not favourably received. The bulk of the remaining saddles were presumably the 1856 'Universal Wood Arch', with the 1860 pattern bridle. Blue cavalry cloaks, with a white lining for officers, were carried strapped over the wallets in front of the saddle. The blue valise, piped white around the ends, bearing '17' above the letter 'L', was strapped behind the saddle, with a mess tin on top.

Dragoon uniforms

Like the Lancers, the Dragoons wore a modified dress uniform, including tunics, but with the foreign service helmet. The officers' tunic was scarlet with blue velvet collar and cuffs, fastened down the front by eight regimental pattern buttons. Lieutenants and captains had a ¾in. band of gold lace around the top of the collar, and field officers had lace all round. Rank badges were worn on either side of the collar opening. The cuffs were edged in gold cord ending in an Austrian knot design—three rows of cord for field officers (extending to 11ins. from the cuff), a double row for captains (extending to 9ins.), and a single row for lieutenants (extending to 7ins.). A gold twisted cord was worn on each shoulder, fastened by two small regimental buttons. There were two further buttons above the centre of the skirts at the rear and three on each shaped panel, which were edged in gold braid. The tunic was piped blue down the front, and the skirts lined white. Breeches were dark blue with a wide gold stripe down the outside, and were reinforced on the inside. Boots were black, with steel spurs. Unlike the Lancers, Dragoon officers seem to have worn an undress pouch belt very similar to the ORs', with a white belt and black pouch. The sword belt was white with a gilt rectangular buckle bearing the regimental badge. The sword itself was the 1856 pattern Heavy Cavalry Officers' Sword, carried in a steel scabbard. Various unofficial brown belts may also have been worn.

The ORs' tunic was also scarlet, with velvet collar, cuffs and shoulder straps. The collar was edged all round with yellow worsted, as were the cuffs, which ended in an Austrian knot device. The shoulder straps were edged in yellow worsted all round except on the seam, and bore '1' and 'DG' in yellow embroidery. The back skirt flaps were edged in yellow and decorated with three buttons. OR's breeches were blue with a wide yellow stripe. The sword belt was white with a snake-clasp, carrying the 1864 pattern sword. Like the Lancers, the Dragoons carried ammunition pouches for their Martini-Henry carbines. No doubt this would have been most uncomfortable after prolonged riding and a photograph of a 1st KDG private visiting Isandlwana in June 1879 suggests a solution—he has his belt casually slung around his shoulder rather than at the waist.

Chelmsford's existing transport was completely inadequate for his needs; civilian wagons, of which this is a typical pattern, were purchased or hired to make up the shortfall. (National Army Museum)

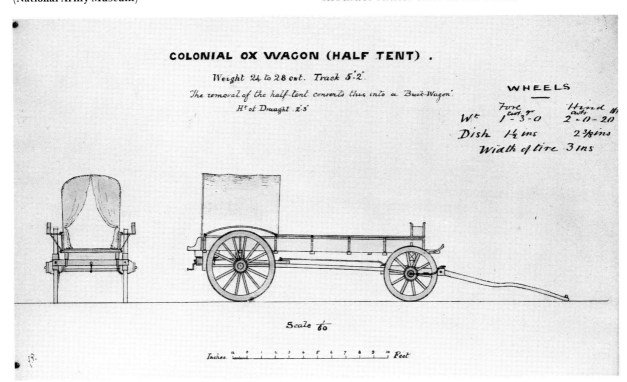

The 17th Lancers encamped at Cato Manor farm, Natal, on their way to the front. Note the lances standing upright between the tents. (Killie Campbell Africana Library).

Artillery

Despite experiments with breech-loading models in the 1860s, the British Army of the 1870s was still primarily armed with muzzle-loading guns. In Zululand, RA batteries were armed with either 7-pdr. or 9-pdr. 8cwt. Rifled Muzzle-Loading guns.

The Mark IV 7-pdr. was intended for use as a mountain gun. It had a steel barrel with three rifling grooves, and a maximum range of 3,100 yards. Designed to be mounted on the small, narrow 'Abyssinian' carriage, it could either be dragged by three mules in tandem, or dismantled and carried on pack mules. Its narrow carriage had advantages in bush country, but it was unstable on more open tracks and easily overturned. As a result, so-called Colonial or Kaffrarian carriages were introduced for use in southern Africa. These were modified versions of the carriage used for the 9-pdr. 8cwt. model. It is sometimes surprisingly difficult to tell from contemporary evidence which guns were used where, but Lt. Lloyd's guns of 11/7 (11 Battery, 7th Brigade), which accompanied Pearson's column and fought at Nyezane, are listed in the official history as 'two 7-pdrs., mule'; whilst N/5, who lost two guns at Isandlwana, had them mounted on Kaffrarian carriages. When mounted on the latter they were drawn by the 16-pdr. Armstrong Limber, which also drew the 9-pounders. Generally, the 7-pdr. did not prove very successful in Zululand. By mounting it on a heavy carriage, much of its chief asset, its manoeuvrability, was lost. It had a low muzzle velocity, which rendered shrapnel largely ineffective, and the small bursting charge meant that the destructive power of the common shell was negligible. On the whole, it was felt that if the 7-pdr. had to be mounted on a 9 pdr. carriage to be practical, they might as well have had the 9-pdr. in the first place.

The 9-pdr. 8cwt. RML was the standard RA field gun of the 1870s, and distinguished itself in the Zulu War, where its contributions to the decisive battles of Khambula and Ulundi were of major importance. The barrel was of wrought-iron, and could throw a shell a maximum of 3,500 yards.

With the many reinforcements who began to arrive at Durban from March onwards came the two Gatlings of 10/7 RA, the first battery in the British Army to have Gatlings. The Gatling was a cumbersome, hand-cranked machine-gun invented by an American, Dr. Richard Gatling, during the Civil War. The British War Office tested the weapon at the beginning of the decade, and was favourably impressed, ordering a number of .45in. Gatlings for Army use and heavy .65in. Gatlings for the Navy.

The artillery version was mounted on a carriage similar to the field guns, and received its rounds from a hopper which fitted above the breech. The British Gatling was designed to take standard

Small Arms ammunition, the Boxer cartridge. This was not entirely suitable, since the soft metal often tore under pressure from the extractor grip, fouling the breech and causing jamming. At Ulundi the bolts slipped out and were hard to find in the long grass, rendering the guns ineffective at a crucial stage of the battle. Nevertheless, when it was working, the Gatling more than made up for its faults. It was ideally suited for use on the open terrain of Zululand against the Zulu massed charge, and those who saw it in action were fascinated by the way it chopped lines clean through the attacking force.

Also used in Zululand were a number of 9-pdr. Hales Rocket Troughs. Rockets had first been used by the British Army during the Napoleonic Wars, where they differed little in principle from an ordinary firework, propelled by a slowly burning charge of black powder. Since a tube is inherently unstable in flight, and will cartwheel over and over, some form of stabilising system is necessary. During the Napoleonic Wars, this was nothing more than a stick, and the range and accuracy of the projectile was barely worth the effort of its invention. During the 1860s, however, William Hale, a mechanic at the Royal Arsenal, invented a stick-less rocket, whose charge ignited through three vents at the base end, where three curved baffles were used to deflect the force and twist the rocket on its central axis. After extensive trials both 9-pdr. and 24-pdr. rockets were approved. The latter were originally intended for siege purposes, but were largely taken up by the Navy, where a tube was developed for on-ship use.

On land the 9-pdr. rockets were launched from a three-legged trough which included an adjustable arm for elevation. The rocket was ignited by means of a friction tube attached to a lanyard and inserted into one of the vents. The gunner firing the rocket had to 'bring ... the lanyard up under the hollow of his left foot, which should be placed close to the hind rest of the trough, and pull ... upwards with his right hand with a steady pull'. What happened next was unpredictable. The elevation system of the trough was intended for use on level ground, and in the field it was difficult to set the range with anything approaching accuracy—a calculation further hindered by the erratic burning rate of the black powder. Rockets were known to sail clear over the heads of their targets or, striking some obstacle, to be deflected wildly off course, even bouncing back at their crew. When they did strike home, they had no warhead as such, and their charge might fail to explode altogether. None the less they were considered useful in Colonial warfare, where the terrifying howl they made in flight, and the sparks and smoke they trailed across the sky, were thought to be of tremendous psychological advantage.

There is no evidence that the Zulus were impressed by them; they never stalled an attack

before one, and simply called them 'paraffin', a white man's combustible material with which they were familiar through the activities of traders. The *Manual of Field Artillery Exercises* specified that 'the (crew) detachment consists of one non-commissioned officer and four gunners'. In fact Maj. Russell's rocket battery, attached to Durnford's No. 2 Column, consisted of one RA bombardier and eight members of the 24th to man three troughs, which were carried on mules. During the battle of Isandlwana they were overrun by the Zulus.

Artillery uniforms

During the Zulu War RA officers seem to have worn the blue patrol jacket almost without exception. This fastened down the front with hooks and eyes and olivets, and was bordered all round with 1in. black mohair braid. There were five rows of flat plait mohair braid across the chest, ending in crow's foot knots and olivets. The cuff was edged in the same braid, ending in crow's foot knots, as were the back seams, which had a knot at each end and two eyes at equal distances. The stand-and-fall collar was edged in wide, flat braid, and no rank badges were worn. Trousers were blue with a 2in. scarlet stripe. Headgear was the inevitable dyed helmet. The sword belt was white with a gilt regimental plate, and photographs indicate that many officers wore leather holster belts, after the manner of the infantry.

Like the infantry, RA rankers seem to have favoured the undress frock; this was dark blue, and fastened by five buttons. The collar was red with yellow worsted piping around the bottom edge; the shoulder straps were piped yellow all round, and the cuff bore a yellow trefoil. The shoulder straps bore the brigade number and a grenade badge embroidered in yellow. NCOs' chevrons were in gold, and sergeants and above had gold

The uniform of an OR of the 1st (King's) Dragoon Guards; an impressive collection displayed at Cardiff Castle. On campaign the brass chin-chain would have been replaced by a leather strap. (Cardiff Castle)

A close-up of the same display, showing the blue cuffs and yellow worsted braid, and details of the sword belt—here without the scabbard. (Cardiff Castle)

10/7 Battery RA, the first Gatling battery in the British Army, with its guns. The two men centre, with chevrons above their cuffs, are staff sergeants. Note the officer in blue patrol. The men appear to be wearing the undress frock. (S Bourquin)

worsted. The OR's frock, which does feature in a few isolated campaign photos, was of a similar pattern, but with nine buttons down the front. It was piped scarlet, and the scarlet collar was edged all round in yellow worsted. The cuffs bore a more ornate Austrian knot design. Shoulder straps were piped scarlet with grenade badge and number in yellow. All rank chevrons were gold lace, and sergeants and above had gold lace instead of worsted. Photographs show NCOs wearing brown leather revolver holsters and sword belts. Regulations specified a white leather belt for ORs with the brass universal locket. Trousers were dark blue with a wide scarlet stripe, and leggings and boots were black.

Departmental Corps

At the start of the war Chelmsford had just one Company of **Royal Engineers**—a theoretical strength of six officers and 194 NCOs and sappers. He received two more in the build-up prior to hostilities, and one final reinforcement after Isandlwana.

Photographs of Engineer officers in the war show them wearing either the blue patrol jacket or the undress frock. The blue patrol had Garter-blue velvet collar and cuffs, and was edged all round with 1in. black mohair braid. It was fastened down the front by hooks and eyes, and there were five double rows of black flat plait mohair across the chest, looping over olivets in the centre, and ending with olivets and crow's foot knots. The cuffs were also edged in the same braid, ending in a crow's foot knot, as were the back seams. The basic design of the RE patrol jacket was very similar to the RA one, the chief distinction being the velvet collar and cuffs.

The officers' undress frock was scarlet with blue velvet collar and cuffs, and fastened by five regimental buttons. The collar was edged all round with narrow gold braid, as was the cuff, ending in a trefoil or crow's foot. There was a thin twist of gold cord on the shoulder, fastened by a small regimental button.

Trousers were dark blue with a wide red stripe, though officers on mounted duties often preferred cord breeches. Headgear was the usual helmet.

1: Infantry private
2: Infantry officer
3: Officer, Royal Artillery
4: Bombardier, Royal Artillery

A

The 1/24th firing line, Isandlwana, 22 January 1879:
1: Sergeant, 24th Regiment
2: Lieutenant, 24th Regiment
3: Private, 24th Regiment
4: Bandsman, 24th Regiment

B

Isandlwana, 22 January 1879:
1: Battalion Quartermaster, 24th Regiment
2: Mounted Infantry private
3: Lt.Col. Anthony Durnford, RE
4: Trooper, Buffalo Border Guard
5: Trooper, Natal Carbineers
6: Trooper, Natal Mounted Police

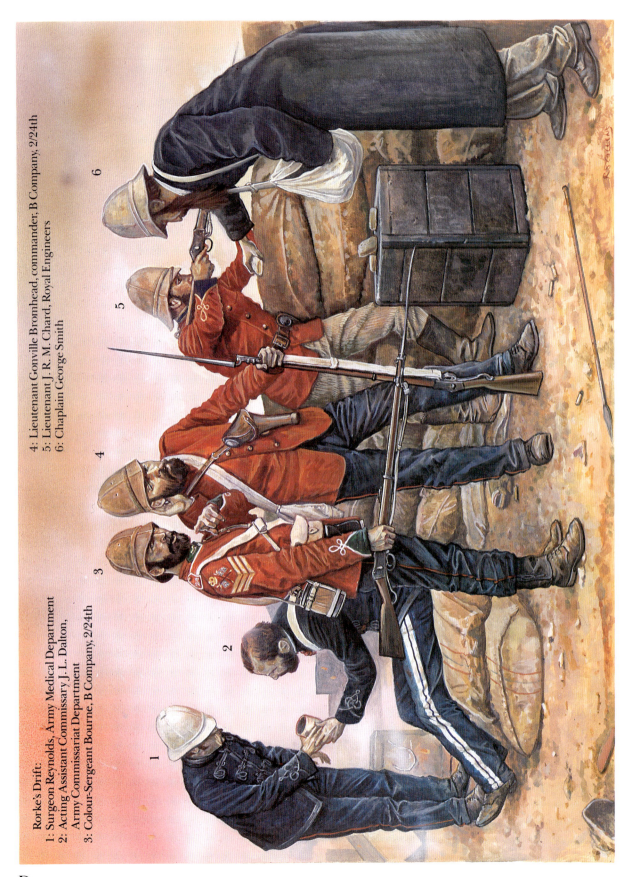

Rorke's Drift:
1: Surgeon Reynolds, Army Medical Department
2: Acting Assistant Commissary J. L. Dalton, Army Commissariat Department
3: Colour-Sergeant Bourne, B Company, 2/24th
4: Lieutenant Gonville Bromhead, commander; B Company, 2/24th
5: Lieutenant J. R. M. Chard, Royal Engineers
6: Chaplain George Smith

The Battle of Nyezane, 22 January 1879:
1: Private, 99th Regiment
2: Sapper, Royal Engineers
3: Trooper, Durban Mounted Rifles
4: Trooper, Stanger Mounted Rifles

1: Private, Army Service Corps
2: Officer, 91st Highlanders
3: Sergeant, 91st Highlanders
4: Private, 91st Highlanders
5: Piper, 91st Highlanders

F

The Naval Brigade at Gingindlovu, 2 April 1879:
1: Sailors, HMS *Boadicea*
2: Private, Royal Marine Light Infantry
3: Officer, Royal Naval landing party
4: Sailor, HMS *Shah*

The descent of the 'Devil's Pass', Battle of Hlobane, 28 March 1879:
1: Trooper, Frontier Light Horse
2: Lt.Col. Redvers Buller
3: Officer, Frontier Light Horse
4: Trooper, Frontier Light Horse
5: Sergeant, Transvaal Volunteers

The death of Lieutenant and Adjutant F. J. Cockaye Frith, 17th Lancers, Upoko River, 5 June 1879:
1: Private, 17th Lancers
2: Corporal, 17th Lancers
3: Lt. and Adj. Frith
4: Officer, 17th Lancers

The Battle of Ulundi, 4 July 1879; inside Lord Chelmsford's square:
1: Privates, Army Hospital Corps
2: Officer, 2/21st Royal Scots Fusiliers
3: Col. Henry Evelyn Wood
4: Lieutenant-General Lord Chelmsford

Natal Native Troops searching the field after Ulundi
1: Trooper, Natal Native Horse
2: Warrior, Natal Native Contingent
3: Swazi Warrior

King Cetshwayo kaMpande in captivity, August 1879:
1: Sergeant, 3/60th Rifles
2: Officer, 3/60th Rifles
3: King Cetshwayo kaMpande
4: Trooper, 1st (King's) Dragoon Guards
5: Major, King's Dragoon Guards

Swords were the 1856 Engineer Officers' pattern, though it seems unlikely, in such a practical profession, that they would have been much carried. No doubt RE officers carried revolvers, field glasses, water-bottles and so on in the same way as infantry officers.

The OR's undress serge was scarlet with blue collar and cuffs. The collar was edged all round with yellow worsted braid, and the cuffs had a single yellow loop. Shoulder cords were of yellow braid held in place by a small button. OR's trousers were dark blue with a red stripe down the outside leg. When on the march infantry-pattern equipment was worn. The men were armed with the Martini-Henry rifle. At the battle of Nyezane sappers of Capt. Wynne's No. 2 Company were improving a river drift while Pearson's column was crossing, when the Zulus attacked. The Zulu left horn advanced rapidly to threaten the drift, and the Engineers were called away to assist in driving them off. At Ulundi Chelmsford used RE men as a reserve within his square, moving them up to support sections of the firing line as they were threatened.

Small detachments from the **Army Hospital Corps** served throughout the war. It was a corps without officers—these being formed separately into the Army Medical Department, though in 1884 the two were brought together and in 1898 amalgamated under the new title of the Royal Army Medical Corps. Typically, the men seem to have worn the undress frock in Zululand. This was dark blue, fastened with five buttons; the collar was piped all round with scarlet braid, as were the shoulder straps. There was a braid trefoil on each cuff, terminating in a curl at each side by the sleeve–back seam, above which were two buttons. The collar badges were brass crowns, and the letters 'AHC', also in brass, were mounted on the shoulder straps. All ranks wore a white arm badge on the right arm, bearing the red cross of Geneva, and edged in gold for senior sergeants and yellow for ORs. Rank chevrons were gold for senior sergeants, and red for lance sergeants and below; they were worn on the right sleeve below the red cross badge. Trousers were dark blue with a narrow red stripe. Gaiters were of the infantry lace-up pattern, and boots were black. Equipment consisted of a brown leather waist belt with snake clasp, with a white haversack and Oliver pattern water-bottle suspended from a brown leather strap. Headgear in the field seems to have been the ubiquitous helmet; or the forage cap, which was peaked, with a gold band, for sergeants only. However, a photograph of a private of the AHC in South Africa in 1879 shows him to be wearing a peaked forage cap, apparently with a white cover.

Information on the **Army Service Corps** at the time of the war is scarce, but there do exist two good photographs of troops in the field. These show at least two different types of jacket, a tunic and an undress frock. The former was dark blue with a blue velvet collar; it was fastened by eight buttons, but was completely plain apart from a white edging to the collar and twisted white shoulder cords (although a number of men in the group have conspicuous white LS & GC chevrons above the right cuff, as well as trade badges). The frock was similar but with a plain blue collar, five buttons, and edging around the collar and shoulder cords. A third pattern of jacket seems to be in evidence, which was plain blue with four buttons—this may have been some sort of working jacket. Forage caps were dark blue with gold button and double gold band for sergeants, and white for lower ranks. Helmets were also worn. Equipment was a brown leather belt with snake-hook fastener; staff sergeants wore swords, and ORs carried sword bayonets.

A 9-pdr. Hales rocket trough, used in Zululand. One arm of the trough is missing, and this rocket seems to be a larger 24-pdr. type. (Natal Museum)

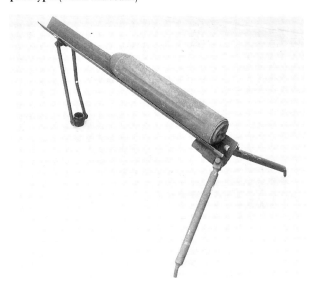

Naval Brigades

Naval Brigade landing parties were a feature of Victorian campaigns and the Zulu War was no exception. The first party was landed by HMS *Active* in November 1878; it was 230 strong, including 34 Royal Marine Light Infantry and eight Royal Marine Artillery. This detachment was present at the reading of the ultimatum to the Zulu envoys at the Lower Drift on 11 December, and subsequently fought with Pearson's Column. A small detachment from HMS *Tenedos* was landed on 1 January 1879; this was only 61 strong, with 15 Marines, including three RMA. In the aftermath of Isandlwana HMS *Shah* was diverted from a homeward journey and landed most of its ship's complement at Durban, a total of 378 men. On 20 March HMS *Boadicea* also landed a brigade of ten officers and 218 men. About 100 Marines were included in the last two detachments. Because, of necessity, Naval Brigades were landed on the coast, they fought throughout the war with the coastal operations.

The uniforms of the sailors seem to have varied slightly between each detachment. The *Active* men appear to have worn blue Navy jumpers with black silk neckerchiefs, white trousers and white caps. The *Tenedos* men wore blue jumpers (their collars are clearly plain and unstriped), neckerchiefs, blue trousers and blue covers to their caps. The *Boadiceas*, however, wore white jumpers with plain white collars and black neckerchiefs, and white trousers, with blue covers over their caps. Only HMS *Shah*'s men seem to have worn straw sennet hats with the name of their ship on a band; they also wore blue jumpers and trousers.

Equipment does seem to have been uniform, however. Canvas leggings with a leather trim were worn by both officers and men. Waist and shoulder belts were brown leather, as were the ammunition pouches. Weapons were the Martini-Henry rifle with a cutlass bayonet, a fearsome looking weapon

Plan of the 9-pdr. RML gun and its carriage, the standard field piece of the Zulu War. The 7-pdr. RML was sometimes mounted on 9-pdr. carriages with very little modification. (Royal Artillery Institute, Woolwich)

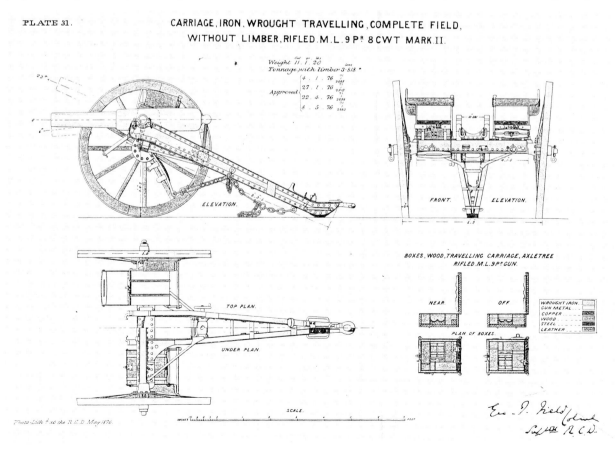

which differed scarcely from the ordinary cutlass except in the provision of fittings to enable it to be attached to the rifle.

Officers wore blue single-breasted jackets with rank indicated by rings around the cuff. Trousers were either blue or white, and headgear was either the peaked cap (blue without a cover, white with), or the ordinary foreign service helmet, dyed brown. Swords were Naval Officers' pattern, carried in black leather scabbards with gilt mounts from a black sword belt. Revolvers worn on shoulder straps also appear common.

The Royal Marine Infantry wore a dark blue working jacket on active service in Zululand. There were four brass buttons down the front, with two small ones retaining twisted scarlet shoulder cords. Collar badges were an embroidered red bugle device. Rank chevrons were worn on both arms, and were gold for senior sergeants and red worsted for below. The uniform of the Royal Marine Artillery differed only in having a grenade badge instead of the bugle and different pattern buttons. Trousers were dark blue with a narrow red stripe for the RMLI and a wide stripe for the RMA. Photographs of Marines in Zululand show the RMLI to be wearing glengarries, and the RMA forage caps. The glengarry was blue with the regimental badge, whilst the forage cap was blue with a yellow band for men and gold for sergeants, and a small grenade badge at front. No doubt in action both would have worn the usual helmet.

Equipment was the 1871 Valise pattern but with black ammunition pouches. The rifle was the Martini-Henry, and all ORs carried the infantry sergeants' pattern sword bayonet. Leggings were black as for infantry. A photograph of Lt. Dowding, RMLI, of the *Active* detachment shows him wearing an infantry-style patrol jacket and blue trousers with a narrow red stripe. He is armed with a regimental pattern sword, and a revolver strap with a conspicuous ammunition pouch.

The Naval detachments brought with them

The 16-pdr. RML limber, used in Zululand to pull the 9-pdr. RML. (Royal Artillery Institute, Woolwich)

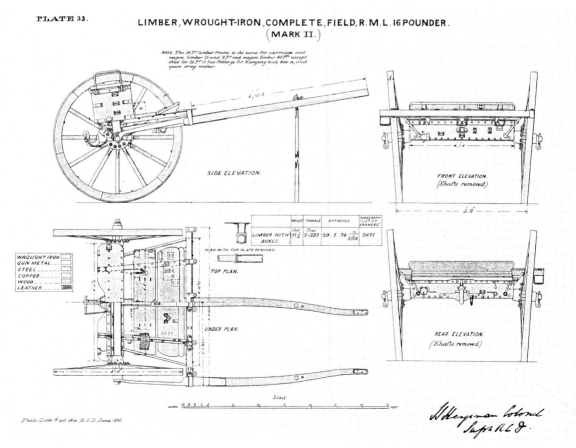

their own artillery, including Gatlings which were used to good effect at Nyezane and Gingindlovu. Unfortunately it is not possible to be certain about the calibre of these guns. Regulations specified .65in. Gatlings for Naval use, but due to a delay in the supply of these the Navy had also acquired a number of Army .45in. calibre weapons. What is certain is that Naval Brigade Gatlings were mounted on different carriages from their Army counterparts, these being narrower and minus the axle-tree boxes. The Navy also landed some of its field guns, including 12-pdr. Armstrongs, but these were replaced by 7-pdrs.—presumably the standard RML model—for the actual advance into Zululand.

They also had a number of Hale's rockets. These were heavy 24-pdrs., fired from tubes rather than the Army's troughs. In 1869 Lt. John Fisher RN had invented a 'sea service rocket tube Mark II'. This was designed to be bracketed onto the side of a ship; but by 1879 a modified version replaced the bracket with a tripod for land service, and the Fisher tube was the type used in Zululand. The 24-pdr. rocket certainly had more power than the 9-pdr. version; and, though it seems to have been just as unpredictable in flight, it scored some notable successes. At Nyezane a well-aimed rocket went right through a homestead occupied by the enemy, setting it on fire, and causing Cdr. Campbell to comment in his report: 'All were remarkably steady under fire ... Boatswain John Cotter was most successful with the rockets I placed in his care.'

Volunteers and Irregulars

On the eve of the Zulu War the Colony of Natal maintained the quasi-military Natal Mounted Police and eight Volunteer units. These had begun to spring up among the settler community in the 1850s when it became clear that the home govern-

Details of the harness equipment used to pull the 16-pdr. RML limber. (Royal Artillery Institute, Woolwich)

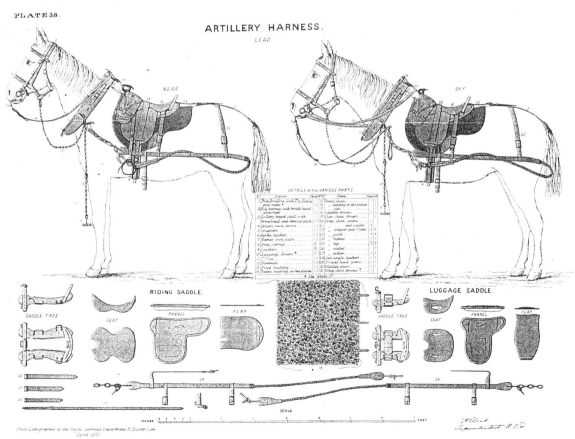

ment would not be prepared to maintain a large permanent garrison in the Colony. The Volunteer movement was stimulated by reports of the Rifle Volunteer Movement at home, although the nature of the country meant that the majority of the units were cavalry rather than infantry. Each unit elected its own officers and provided its own uniforms, whilst the government provided weapons and ammunition.

The Natal Mounted Police, a permanent police force used to regulate the behaviour of both black and white inhabitants of Natal, and the closest thing the Colony had to regular troops, was only 80 strong in 1879, and most of the Volunteer units were smaller: 20 for the Alexandra Mounted Rifles, 38 for the Buffalo Border Guard, 40 for the Stanger Mounted Rifles. In the main these volunteers were enthusiastic; they met to train regularly, they were often good shots and good horsemen, and they were certainly used to the country, so their military value outweighed their paucity of numbers, especially in a force chronically short of cavalry. Uniforms varied from unit to unit, but dark blue or black braided uniforms were popular, with forage caps or helmets, whose fittings seem to have been retained on active service.

From the moment plans were announced by the War Office to introduce Swinburne-Henry carbines amongst regular troops the authorities in Natal campaigned vigorously to be allowed to issue them to their Volunteers. They were told that regular troops had priority and that they would have to wait. Instead they received a Snider carbine, of a pattern with a particularly short stock (presumably to reduce the weight and facilitate use from the saddle). By the time the war with the Zulus loomed, however, the home government relented, and the Sniders were replaced by Swinburne-Henrys—again with shorter stocks than on the standard model—just before the start of the campaign. NCOs and officers also carried swords, and ORs a Bowie knife which could be attached to the end of the carbine to form a

Plans of the .45in. Royal Artillery Gatling, its carriage and limber (Royal Artillery Institute, Woolwich)

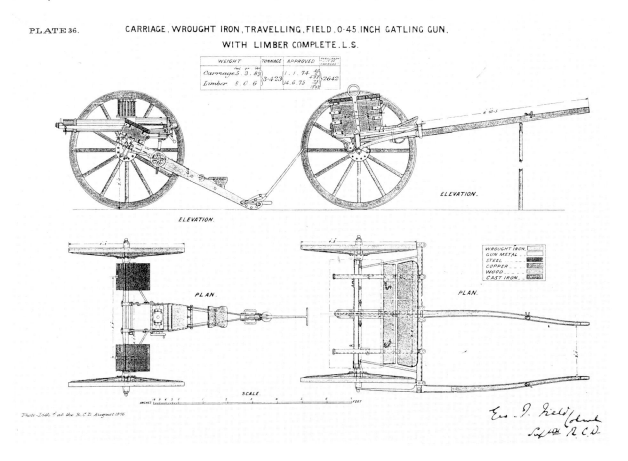

bayonet. Equipment also seems to have been issued centrally, and consisted of brown leather ammunition belt and pouch and a white haversack.

It is worth noting that the Natal Volunteers had been enlisted for the defence of Natal, and could not technically be employed outside the borders of the Colony. The Lieutenant-Governor of Natal, Sir Henry Bulwer, the senior administrator of the province, was deeply opposed to the Zulu War, and constantly tried to thwart Chelmsford's plans whenever they interacted with Natal's administrative system. He insisted that Chelmsford allow the Volunteers to vote on whether they would serve in Zululand. They did.

In addition to the Natal Volunteer units, Chelmsford had at his disposal a number of Irregular cavalry units. Unlike the Volunteers these were not men who were part of an existing system, but who simply joined up for a short period of service instead. Perhaps the most famous of these were the Frontier Light Horse, a unit some 200 strong originally raised on the Eastern Cape Frontier. They seem to have started out in smart uniforms, though details are scarce and contradictory. They seem to have worn buff cord jackets with several rows of narrow braid across the chest, ending in a trefoil knot. Trousers were black with a red stripe. A second uniform existed which was of black cord with flat black mohair edging, and black braid around the cuffs. This may have been worn by officers, although photographs exist of Sgt. O'Toole, VC, and Trooper Brown, DCM, both wearing it. (However, this may reflect a desire to look smart for the camera rather than general practice.) Equipment consisted of a bandolier and carbine. By the time the Zulu War broke out most men were wearing civilian clothes with a red puggaree around the hat.

Of the other Irregular units it is very difficult to be sure. Those raised in the Transvaal were issued riding breeches, boots, a jacket, a hat with a puggaree, and a carbine and bandolier. The puggaree was probably red, or possibly white, a colour favoured in the Transvaal, and the jacket almost certainly a dark brown civilian type. Uniform details were minimal—ranks were probably indicated by white tape chevrons. There was certainly no provision for replacement clothing once it became worn out, so no doubt civilian items would have been substituted.

Finally, Evelyn Wood's Column had the service of the Boer leader Piet Uys. Most Boers along the Zululand border were hard-line republicans, bitterly anti-British, and content to see them slog it

Royal Naval detachment from HMS *Tenedos* on top of Fort Pearson, overlooking the Lower Drift of the Thukela, with Gatling (left) and limber (right). The Navy Gatling was mounted on a narrower carriage than the RA version, without the axle-tree boxes. The sailor centre is carrying an ammunition hopper. (Local History Museum, Durban)

Officers and men from HMS *Tenedos'* Naval Brigade, wearing blue uniform with blue covers on their caps, and brown leather equipment. Note the Marines, right, in frocks and glengarries. (Africana Museum, Johannesburg)

out with their old enemies the Zulus; Boer support for the British invasion was therefore minimal. However, Piet Uys, a respected farmer in the 'disputed territory' on the Transvaal/Zululand border, whose family had a history of struggle against the Zulus, did come forward with 32 of his family and followers. They fought at Hlobane, where unfortunately Uys was killed. His men were disheartened and returned to their farms the next day, taking no further part in the campaign.

Natal's African Troops

When the first whites arrived in Natal in the 1820s the area was largely depopulated by the persistent raiding of the Zulu king Shaka. Once the whites had secured an official title to the land the survivors of these raids began to return, and the land began to fill up. This process was accelerated over the years by vast numbers of refugees fleeing successive political crises within Zululand itself. By the eve of the Zulu War Natal's black population was over 300,000. Many of these had a traditional hostility towards the Zulus which made them potentially good recruits for Chelmsford's army. The Lieutenant-Governor, Sir Henry Bulwer, was opposed to the idea of raising levy units, realising that it might sour relations between Natal blacks and the neighbouring Zulus for generations; and a sector of Colonial society was always worried about arming the African population because of the danger of revolt. Chelmsford overcame Bulwer's objections and was able to raise three regiments of the Natal Native Contingent, but the issue of black troops remained a contentious one throughout the war.

The 1st Regiment, NNC, had three battalions, and the other two regiments two each. Each battalion consisted of ten companies of nine European NCOs and 100 levies. Any promise the regiments may have had, however, was largely vitiated through lack of money. It had been hoped to issue each man with a red coat, but this proved impractical, so the universal badge of African troops became a red rag around the head. The men were also issued with blankets and woollen comforter caps, and many turned out in items of cast-off European clothing. Only one in ten was issued with a firearm, often of obsolete pattern, and ammunition was limited to a few rounds to prevent wastage. For the most part the men carried their own shields and spears, though there is a tantalising (if unconfirmed) reference to pikes being issued. Companies also seem to have improvised their own flags.

Officers were drawn largely from Imperial regiments, or from settlers with some experience of command, and wherever possible staff officers, at least, spoke Zulu. The NCOs were generally of poor calibre, since many of the better volunteers had already joined the more prestigious mounted units. Those who remained were often European immigrants who spoke little English and less Zulu, and who treated their men with contempt. Most

Members of the Natal Carbineers (left) and Natal Native Horse, in camp c.1879. The general appearance of the NNH men is well conveyed. The man in white (right) may be a member of the magistrate's black police (Natal Archives)

NNC officers wore infantry-style patrol jackets, riding breeches, and a wide-brimmed hat with a red puggaree—a uniform popular with officers throughout the Irregular units. It is difficult to be certain what the NCOs wore; they appear in photographs with dark, probably brown, jackets, cord trousers, and hats.

The reputation of the NNC has suffered unfairly at the hands of historians, largely because it received an undue amount of blame for the Isandlwana débâcle. Well led and intelligently employed, much could have been made of it. Its primary duties were scouting and mopping up after a battle, and at these it excelled; it was never intended as front-line material. After Isandlwana the 3rd Regiment was so badly shaken that it was disbanded, and the remaining regiments were reorganised into independent battalions. Belatedly, they were given a higher proportion of firearms.

Rather more successful from the first were five troops of mounted blacks, each of about 50 men, known collectively as the Natal Native Horse. Three of these troops were drawn from the amaNgwane clan, who lived in the Drakensburg foothills in Natal and who were old enemies of the Zulus. They were known to the British as the Sikhali Horse after their Chief Zikhali. One of the other troops was composed of Tlokwa Basothos, led by Hlubi Molife, an old friend of Col. Durnford. The last one was drawn from the black Christian community at Edendale. All the NNH wore European clothing with a red rag round their hats. Most preferred to ride barefoot, with their toes grasping the stirrup, but the Edendale men were booted and spurred. All were armed with carbines, and some carried hide quivers of assegais behind their saddles.

One unit which was uniformed was the Natal Native Pioneers. This was 273 strong, divided into five companies, the companies being distributed amongst the columns during the first invasion. The Pioneers carried carbines as well as picks and shovels, and seem to have been given the old 1872 pattern frock with the single loop of braid on the cuffs, and the collar torn out. The trousers were white canvas and extended to the knee only. Forage caps appear to have been blue with a white band.

In addition to the NNC Chelmsford also organised less permanent black units for border defence. A small number of black policemen kept an eye on the major river crossings on behalf of district magistrates. There are tantalising references to them being uniformed, and they may have worn a white canvas shirt and trousers; they were armed with old percussion rifles. Border Guards, raised from clans living along the frontier and placed under white levy-leaders, were stationed in companies of 100, with 200 more in reserve, near the more important drifts. Finally, there was a Border Levy, again drawn from local clans, who were expected to turn out to defend their district should the Zulus attack. All of these men carried their own weapons, and at the most wore no more uniform than a red headband. White levy-leaders, often border magistrates or men well used to the area, improvised their own uniforms to achieve a military look, patrol jackets of various patterns being popular.

In the northern theatre Wood was able to recruit both friendly Zulus and Swazi warriors. The Zulus were mostly followers of the Zulu prince Hamu kaNzibe, who defected to the British with his followers. They were drafted into a unit known as Wood's Irregulars, along with a number of Swazis. The Swazis, who lived north of Zululand, were traditional enemies of the Zulus and were content to join the war in the hope of plunder. Both photographs and engravings indicate that they wore their full ceremonial regalia into action.

British Columns in Zululand, 1879

First Invasion

Number One Column (Colonel Pearson)
Royal Artillery, 2 7-pdrs.
Royal Engineers, No. 2 Company
2nd Battalion, 3rd Foot
99th Foot (6 companies)
Naval Brigade
No. 2 Squadron, Mounted Infantry
Natal Hussars
Durban Mounted Rifles
Alexandra Mounted Rifles
Stanger Mounted Rifles
Victoria Mounted Rifles
2nd Regiment, Natal Native Contingent
(2 battalions)
Natal Native Pioneers, No. 2 Company

Number Two Column (Lt. Col. Durnford)
Rocket Battery
1st Regiment, Natal Native Contingent
(3 battalions)

NCOs of the Durban Mounted Rifles. They are carrying Snider carbines, which were replaced just before the Zulu War with Swinburne-Henrys. (Natal Archives)

A family reunion in the Natal Volunteer Corps on the eve of the Zulu War: Lt. W. E. Shepstone (seated left) and fellow officers of the Durban Mounted Rifles are visited by his brother, 'Offy' Shepstone of the Natal Carbineers (seated right). The man in the foreground is also a Carbineer officer, and both are wearing the NC's braided blue patrol jacket with white facings. (Natal Archives)

Sikali Horse
Natal Native Pioneers, No. 3 Company

Number Three Column (Colonel Glyn)

N/5 Battery, Royal Artillery (7-pdrs.)
Royal Engineers, No. 5 Company
1st Battalion, 24th Foot
2nd Battalion, 24th Foot
No. 1 Squadron, Mounted Infantry
Natal Mounted Police
Natal Carbineers
Newcastle Mounted Rifles
Buffalo Border Guard
3rd Regiment, Natal Native Contingent
(2 battalions)
Natal Native Pioneers, No. 2 Company

Number Four Column (Colonel Wood)

11/7 Battery, Royal Artillery (7-pdrs.)
1st Battalion, 13th Foot
90th Foot
Frontier Light Horse
Wood's Irregulars

Note: following the disaster at Isandlwana a number of Irregular units were transferred to this Column from No. 5 Column. Several other units (Boer Volunteers, Baker's Horse, Kaffrarian Rifles) joined this Column during the course of the First Invasion.

Number Five Column (Colonel Rowlands)

80th Foot
Schutte's Corps
Eckersley's Contingent
Raaf's Corps
Ferreira's Horse
Border Horse
One Krupp gun, two 6-pdr. Armstrongs

Second Invasion

First Division (Major-General H. H. Crealock)

1st Brigade
2nd Battalion, 3rd Foot (8 companies)
88th Foot (6 companies)
99th Foot (8 companies)
2nd Brigade
57th Foot (8 companies)
3 Battalion, 60th Rifles (7 companies)
91st Highlanders (8 companies)
Divisional troops
Naval Brigade, with 3 guns
4th Battalion, Natal Native Contingent
5th Battalion, Natal Native Contingent
John Dunn's Scouts
Natal Volunteers (as per original No. 1 Column)
M/6 Battery, RA (7-pdrs.)
8/7 Battery, RA (2 7-pdrs.)
11/7 Battery, RA (2 7-pdrs.)
0/6 Battery, RA (Ammunition Column)
Royal Engineers, 30th Company

Second Division (Major-General Newdigate)

1st Brigade
2nd Battalion, 21st Foot (6 companies)
58th Foot (6 companies)
2nd Brigade
1st Battalion, 24th Foot (7 companies)
94th Foot (6 companies)
Divisional Troops
N/5 Battery, RA (7-pdrs.)
N/6 Battery (9-pdrs.)
0/6 Battery, RA (Ammunition Column)
Royal Engineers, No. 2 Company
Bettington's Natal Horse
Shepstone's Basothos
2nd Battalion, Natal Native Contingent
Army Service Corps
Army Medical Department
Cavalry Brigade
(Attached to 2nd Division)
1st Dragoon Guards
17th Lancers

Flying Column (Brigadier-General Wood)
1st Battalion, 13th Foot
80th Foot
90th Foot

Men of the Stanger Mounted Rifles (with large badges on their forage caps) and Victoria Mounted Rifles. The VMR's uniform was dark blue with red facings, including a red band around their forage caps. The influence of the British Rifle Volunteer Movement on these men's uniforms is very clear (Natal Archives)

11/7 Battery, RA (4 7-pdrs.)
10/7 Battery, RA (Gatlings)
Royal Engineers, No. 5 Company
Mounted Infantry
Frontier Light Horse
Transvaal Rangers
Baker's Horse
Natal Native Horse
Natal Native Pioneers
Natal Light Horse
Wood's Irregulars

Note: this list gives the nominal strength of each column at the start of the First and Second Invasions, and does not reflect the order of battle in individual engagements. A complete list of all British troop dispositions, including details of specific engagements, troops deployed on lines of communications, reinforcements and reorganisations, can be found in the official history, the *Narrative of Field Operations Connected with the Zulu War of 1879* (HMSO, 1881, reprinted 1907, 1989).

The Plates

A1: Infantry private
Wearing a greatcoat and based on sketches by Lt. W. W. Lloyd, 24th Regt. Lloyd shows men in greatcoats on wet days or on night picket duty. Blankets were worn *en banderole* with light equipment; a waist belt with one ammunition pouch, and haversack.

A2: Infantry officer
He is also in a greatcoat, again after Lloyd. The officers' greatcoats were double-breasted, and the sword and revolver belt were apparently worn over the top.

A3: Officer, Royal Artillery
This figure is based on a portrait of Maj. F. B. Russell, who was killed in action commanding the rocket battery at Isandlwana. He is wearing a typical RA officer's uniform; the blue patrol jacket with revolver carried by a shoulder strap, and sword.

A4: Bombardier, Royal Artillery
The rocket battery was manned at Isandlwana by one bombardier and eight privates from the 24th. This man is wearing the OR's undress frock, and is explaining the system of the 9-pdr. rocket trough. The rockets themselves were painted red and the launchers black.

B: The 1/24th firing line, Isandlwana, 22 January 1879:
B1: Sergeant, 24th Regiment
This figure is wearing the undress frock and typical 'fighting kit'—the waist belt with buff ammunition pouches and black expense pouch at rear, and haversack and water-bottle. The chevrons for Line regiments are worn on the right sleeve only. Note the bullock-hide guard sewn over the stock to protect the left hand from an over-heated barrel. Although Queen's Regulations stated that only

A self-portrait by Lt. W. Fairlie showing his uniform as an officer in the Natal Native Horse. He is wearing a blue infantry patrol jacket, buff riding breeches, and a slouch hat with a red puggaree—a uniform favoured by many Irregular officers. (National Army Museum)

Commandant Piet Uys (centre) and his sons. Uys was the only Boer leader to support the British invasion of Zululand; he was killed at the battle of Hlobane. (S. Bourquin)

moustaches were to be worn, this was relaxed on campaign where full beards were the norm.

B2: Lieutenant, 24th Regiment
Wearing the officers' undress serge, demonstrates it was common practice for only field officers and above to wear rank badges on the collar, and in the 24th junior officers wore a regimental badge instead.

B3: Private, 24th Regiment
Again, he is wearing the undress frock, with Long Service and Good Conduct chevrons on the right sleeve, and a 'marksman' badge on the other, reflecting the experience of many of the 1st Battalion men.

B4: Bandsman, 24th
Bandsmen were used as stretcher bearers in battle. Band uniforms were apparently unique to each battalion, some having quite ornate uniforms, others ordinary tunics or frocks. This winged tunic with bandsman's badge is based on photographs of the 1/24th's band in King William's Town in 1878. The cap is the standard glengarry with regimental badge.

C: Isandlwana, 22 January 1879:
C1: Battalion Quartermaster, 24th Regiment
Each infantry battalion had a Quartermaster, a commissioned officer who had risen through the ranks. He was usually given an honorary rank, often lieutenant; as such he would have worn the same uniform as his fellow officers, with the exception of the black leather belt. In this case he is wearing a forage cap and the blue, infantry pattern patrol jacket. No doubt, like other officers, he might also have carried a revolver.

C2: Mounted Infantry private
The MI were made up of infantrymen drawn from a number of battalions, who wore their regimental serge (this man is from the 80th) with cord riding breeches. The carbine is the Swinburne-Henry.

C3: Lt. Col. Anthony Durnford, RE
Durnford was one of the British commanders at Isandlwana and was killed with one of the 'last stands'. This is based on his own description of his service uniform. He is wearing an Engineer officer's patrol jacket with rank badges. His left arm, disabled by a wound years before, is tucked into his jacket. He wears a wide-brimmed hat with red puggaree, reflecting his command of black troops, and riding breeches.

C4: Trooper, Buffalo Border Guard
One of the Natal Volunteer units, the BBG, who fought at Isandlwana, wore a black cord uniform which, unlike its counterpart in the Natal Mounted Police, retained its colour. For undress troopers wore a black forage cap with a distinctive buffalo-head badge, but it seems likely that in action they wore the helmet with full fittings.

C5: Trooper, Natal Carbineers
The premier Natal Volunteer unit, the Carbineers wore a blue uniform with white facings. The officers' tunics had five rows of black lace across the front, ending in trefoil knots, and no buttons.

C6: Trooper, Natal Mounted Police
The NMP's uniform was also black, though the dye seems to have been unable to withstand the rigours of field use, and there are several references to the uniform fading to brown. Note the carbine bayonet. Officers and NCOs carried swords.

D: Rorke's Drift:
D1: Surgeon Reynolds, Army Medical Department
Reynolds was in charge of the hospital at Rorke's Drift, and during the battle greatly distinguished himself tending the wounded. We have shown him wearing the AMD's patrol jacket, which was of infantry pattern, and have assumed that he would have worn the foreign service helmet.

D2: Acting Assistant Commissary J. L. Dalton, Army Commissariat Department
Dalton was one of the Commissary staff in charge of the supply depot before the fight. He played an active role in planning the defences, and was wounded whilst manning the barricades. He later returned to the fight to hand out ammunition. He is wearing the infantry pattern patrol jacket and undress trousers, which had a double white stripe down the outside seam.

D3: Colour-Sergeant Bourne, B Company, 2/24th
Colour-Sergeant Bourne received the DCM for his part in the defence. Based on contemporary company photographs, our reconstruction shows him

wearing the undress frock with colour sergeant's chevrons.

D4: Lieutenant Gonville Bromhead, commander, B Company, 2/24th
Based on contemporary photographs; we show him wearing an OR's serge stripped of all insignia except the collar patches. He is known to have used both a rifle and a revolver during the fight.

D5: Lieutenant J. R. M. Chard, Royal Engineers
Chard was the senior officer at Rorke's Drift. Based on a careful sifting of the evidence, we have reconstructed him in an undress frock with riding breeches. Like Bromhead, he is known to have used both a revolver and a rifle during the fight, the former presumably his own, the latter probably a 24th spare.

D6: Chaplain George Smith
Smith was the vicar of Escourt in Natal, who had accompanied the Centre Column to Rorke's Drift. During the battle he went the rounds handing out ammunition, and exhorting the men not to swear. He wore a long black civilian coat, faded to green, and distributed cartridges from a haversack.

E: The Battle of Nyezane, 22 January 1879:
E1: Private, 99th Regiment
Photographs show that the 99th wore the old-style 1872 pattern frock with single-loop cuff design.

Capt. Cecil D'Arcy, VC (left), and Sgt. Edmund O'Toole, VC, of the Frontier Light Horse. D'Arcy is wearing a typical Irregular officers' uniform, while O'Toole is wearing the FLH's black uniform. (Kille Campbell Africana Library)

Since Pearson's column was attacked on the march, we have shown him in full marching order. Note that this battalion also had black ammunition pouches instead of the more common buff type.

E2: Sapper, Royal Engineers
The Engineers were working to improve the riving crossing when the battle began, and were rushed up to assist in driving back the Zulu left horn. This

Unfortunately in poor condition, this fascinating photograph shows men of the Natal Native Horse at Sir Garnet Wolseley's camp at Ulundi in September 1879 at the end of the Zulu War. Most are wearing slouch hats with puggarees, though one (centre) has a forage cap, and another (right) has a Zulu-style leopard-skin headband around his hat. The officers at centre are from the Mounted Infantry and Natal Mounted Police. (John Young Collection)

man is wearing the undress frock with infantry-pattern pouches.

E3: *Trooper, Durban Mounted Rifles*
The DMR wore one of the most colourful Volunteer uniforms with red trim and black braid. Officers wore a similar uniform but with crow's foot knots on the tunic braid and olivets down the front. They carried swords and revolvers.

E4: *Trooper, Stanger Mounted Rifles*
One of the units which most reflected the influence of the Rifle Volunteer movement, the SMR was 40 strong and served with Pearson's column. When the siege of Eshowe began all the Volunteer units present were sent back to Natal; they later accompanied the relief column, and fought at Gingindlovu.

F1: *Private, Army Service Corps*
This private is in undress frock and forage cap. Photographs indicate that the helmet was also widely worn.

F2: *Officer, 91st Highlanders*
He is wearing the undress frock which had the facing colour on the collar only, and 'veld boots'. His equipment is the regimental pattern sword belt, and usual holster and other belts.

F3: *Sergeant, 91st Highlanders*
The sergeant appears in full marching order. This shows the usual method of wearing the Valise equipment: rolled greatcoat at the top, mess-tin, and expense pouch at the bottom. The valise itself is not carried. Note that Highland NCOs wore chevrons on both sleeves.

F4: *Private, 91st Highlanders*
He is wearing the serge frock, and a blanket *en banderole*, as seems to have been popular with this battalion. Note that the ammunition pouches on the waist belt are black rather than buff.

Although this sketch represents the campaign against Sekhukhune in late 1879, it gives an excellent impression of the appearance of the Irregulars from the Transvaal, and of the Swazis, who seem to have fought in their full ceremonial regalia in both campaigns. (Author's Collection)

Maj. Bengough's 2/1st NNC outside Fort Bengough in Natal during the Zulu War. Most of the men have no uniform except a red rag around their heads, though many are wearing items of European clothing. (Natal Archives)

F5: *Piper, 91st Highlanders*
Based on a photograph of the battalion on the march, he is wearing the undress regimental piper's uniform, with the valise equipment behind.

G: *The Naval Brigade at Gingindlovu, 2 April 1879:*
G1: *Sailor, HMS Boadicea.*
The men from the *Boadicea*'s detachment wore white jumpers, trousers and caps. All belts are brown. The rocket equipment is the Fisher launching tube Mark II, for the 24-pdr. Hales rocket. Originally intended for use aboard ship, the Fisher tube was adapted for land service by the addition of a tripod.

G2: *Private, Royal Marine Light Infantry*
He is wearing the blue working jacket adopted on this campaign, with valise equipment with black ammunition pouches.

G3: *Officer, Royal Naval landing party*
Most Royal Navy officers, whatever their detachment, seem to have favoured the blue jacket, with either white or blue trousers, and the cap. Revolvers were carried as per infantry officers.

G4: *Sailor, HMS Shah*
Sketches and engravings of the *Shah*'s men during the battle show them to have worn blue trousers and jumpers, canvas leggings, and straw 'sennet' hats. Note the cutlass bayonet on the Martini-Henry.

H: *The descent of the 'Devil's Pass', Battle of Hlobane, 28 March 1879:*
H1: *Trooper, Frontier Light Horse*
Pieced together from confusing contemporary evidence, this shows the FLH's original uniform; a buff braided jacket with black trousers. Some men would still have been wearing this in Zululand, whilst others simply wore civilian clothes with a red rag around the hat. All, however, would have carried a carbine and bandolier.

H2: *Lt. Col. Redvers Buller*
Wood's dynamic cavalry commander, Buller won the VC for rescuing men in the débâcle at Hlobane. Sketches show that he fought in a practical civilian costume of Norfolk jacket and riding breeches.

H3: *Officer, Frontier Light Horse*
Many Irregular officers, of whatever unit, preferred to wear the infantry-style patrol jacket, with cord riding breeches, and a wide-brimmed hat with puggaree. Certainly Cecil D'Arcy, who won the VC with the FLH at Ulundi, was pictured in this uniform. Most Irregular officers would also have been armed with both a carbine and revolver.

H4: *Trooper, Frontier Light Horse*
Based on contemporary photographs, this shows the FLH's black cord uniform—though the exact significance of this uniform remains a mystery.

H5: *Sergeant, Transvaal Volunteers*
Many of the Irregular units who fought with Wood—Raaf's Transvaal Rangers, the Kaffrarian Rifles, the Border Horse—probably wore little

A 7-pdr. RML gun used in the Zulu War, mounted on a 'Kaffrarian' carriage, a modified version of the 9-pdr. carriage. (S A Museum of Military History, Johannesburg).

more than civilian dress with a coloured puggaree around the hat. If NCO ranks were indicated at all, they were probably marked with white worsted tape.

I: The death of Lieutenant and Adjutant F. J. Cockaye Frith, 17th Lancers, Upoko River, 5 June 1879:

I1: Private, 17th Lancers
This shows the full extent of campaign modifications: the dyed helmet, reversed plastron tunic front, and ammunition pouches worn with the sword belt.

I2: Corporal, 17th Lancers
This corporal clearly shows the detail of the rear of the tunic and equipment. Note that the sword is hooked up to a small hook on the sword belt.

I3: Lt. and Adj. Frith.
Frith was killed in a skirmish on the Upoko in early June and is shown wearing the dress tunic, with plastron reversed, and lieutenant's rank insignia. Note the leather revolver belt worn with the full dress pouch belt. Most illustrations show officers' tunics at this period to have round collars; Frith is unusual in that contemporary portraits clearly show him with a square collar.

I4: Officer, 17th Lancers
As well as the dress tunic, some officers wore patrol jackets. Unlike the infantry, cavalry patrol jackets varied from regiment to regiment. This is the type favoured by the 17th.

J: The Battle of Ulundi, 4 July 1879; inside Lord Chelmsford's square:

J1: Privates, Army Hospital Corps
The AHC seem to have worn both helmets and forage caps on campaign in Zululand; the cap with the white cover is based on a contemporary photo. The jackets are the undress frock; note the distinctive red cross badge (right arm only).

J2: Officer, 2/21st Royal Scots Fusiliers
Although a Scottish regiment the 21st's uniform was largely the same as for Line Infantry; compare this with Fig.B2. One feature of the 21st officers' frock was that it had shoulder cords rather than straps, and the grenade badge was always worn on the collar. The cuff rank distinction is for major. The officers of this battalion also retained the grenade helmet badge, but not the ORs.

J3: Col. Henry Evelyn Wood
Wood commanded the Flying Column troops during the battle. He is wearing the frock of his regiment, the 90th LI, with colonel's rank distinctions; and a dyed helmet rather than the one with elaborate fittings with which he posed for photographs.

J4: Lieutenant-General Lord Chelmsford
He is in his field service kit, a blue patrol jacket with riding breeches, and a helmet with a plain puggaree.

Several regiments which took part in the battle did so with Colours flying. Those in the background are of the 1/13th Light Infantry, with the Queen's Colour to the fore.

K: Natal Native troops searching the field after Ulundi:
K1: Trooper, Natal Native Horse
The NNH wore European clothing with a red rag around their hats. Most preferred to ride barefoot.

They were armed with carbines, and sometimes with spears carried in a holster at the back of the saddle.

K2: Warrior, Natal Native Contingent
He is wearing his issued blanket and red distinguishing rag around the head, with a mixture of European and African clothing. The weapons are his own shield and spear.

K3: Swazi Warrior
Sketches show that the Swazis wore their full regalia into action. This magnificent costume consists of a 'busby' of trimmed ostrich feathers, with *sakabuli* feathers on either side, and streamers of feathers hanging below the otter-skin headband. His body is covered with cow-tail ornaments, and around his waist he wears a skirt of animal skin.

L: King Cetshwayo kaMpande in captivity, August 1879:
L1: Sergeant, 3/60th Rifles
The 60th's uniform was extremely sombre, the rifle green of the jacket and trousers in fact being black. All equipment was of black leather, including the sling on the rifle. Rifle regiments wore chevrons on both sleeves, and all ORs carried the sword bayonet.

L2: Officer, 3/60th Rifles
He is wearing the undress frock. Being less conspicuous than their Line counterparts, the 60th retained their helmet plates but dyed the helmets brown.

L3: King Cetshwayo kaMpande
When the king was captured by a patrol of the KDG he was wearing a table-cloth as a cloak. He looked haggard after his ordeal, but accepted his fate with dignity. He was carrying a staff which had once belonged to his great uncle, King Shaka, the founder of the Zulu nation.

L4: Trooper, 1st (King's) Dragoon Guards
Like the Lancers, the Dragoons on campaign carried ammunition pouches with their waist belts, as well as a pouch belt and haversack.

L5: Major, King's Dragoon Guards
This officer is wearing the dress tunic with major's rank distinctions, but with the undress pouch belt and sword belt.

A 9-pdr. RML gun used in the Zulu War. (SA Museum of Military History, Johannesburg).

Notes sur les planches en couleur

A1 Soldat d'infanterie en manteau; couverture en banderole; équipement léger, un ceinturon, un sac à munitions, et musette. **A2** Officier d'infanterie en manteau croisé; ceinturon pour épée et révolver. **A3** Officier de l'Artillerie Royale en veste de patrouille bleue avec révolver sur la bandoulière et épée. **A4** Bombardier de l'Artillerie Royale en tunique de petite tenue dans les autres grades.

B1 Sergent, 24ème Régiment, en tunique de petite tenue et "ensemble de combat". Notez le pontet en peau sur le fusil. **B2** Lieutenant portant l'habit de petite tenue en serge des officiers avec écusson du régiment sur le col. **B3** Soldat en tunique de petite tenue avec chevrons de Long Service et Bonne Conduite sur la manche droite et écusson de tireur d'élite sur l'autre. **B4** Des musiciens furent utilisés pour porter les brancards en combat. Celui-ci porte un uniforme d'Orchestre, qui était unique à chaque bataillon, et un glengarry.

C1 Officier chargé des vivres et des fournitures en calot et veste de patrouille bleue avec ceinturon à poche de cuir. **C2** Soldat d'infanterie montée portant l'habit de serge et des culottes de cheval en velours; la carabine est une

Farbtafeln

A1 Ein Infanteriesoldat mit Mantel; Decke en banderole, leichte Ausrüstung, ein Hüftgürtel, eine Munitionstasche und eine Provianttasche. **A2** Infanterieoffizier mit doppelreihigem Mantel; Schwert- und Revolvergürtel. **A3** Offizier der Royal Artillery mit blauer Patrouillenjacke, Revolver am Schulterriemen befestigt, sowie mit Schwert ausgerüstet. **A4** Kanonier der Royal Artillery, gekleidet im Interimsrehrock eines anderen Ranges.

B1 Sergeant des 24. Regiments mit Interimsgehrock und "Kampfausrüstung". Zu beachten ist der Gewehrschutz aus Ochsenleder. **B2** Ein Leutnant, der hier mit einem Offiziers-Interims-Serge bekleidet ist, das am Kragen das Regimentsabzeichen zeigt. **B3** Ein Soldat im Interimsgehrock mit Winkelabzeichen auf dem rechten Ärmel für lange Dienstzeit und gute Führung, sowie das "Scharfschützen-Abzeichen" am anderen Arm. **B4** Mitglieder der Musikkapelle wurden bei Kämpfen zum Tragen von Krankentragen herangezogen. In der Abbildung ist er in der Musikkappelleuniform gekleidet, die von Bataillon zu Bataillon anders war. Darüber hinaus hat er die Mütze der Hochlandschotten auf.

Swinburne-Henry. **C3** Le Lt Col Anthony Durnford RE dans une veste de patrouille d'officier du génie et un chapeau à bord large avec un voile rouge. **C4** Soldat de la cavalerie, du Buffalo Border Guard, l'une des unités de Volontaires du Natal, dans l'uniforme en velours noir. **C5** Les Carabiniers du Natal portaient un uniforme blue avec des parements blancs. **C6** La Police Montée du Natal portait un uniforme noir qui avait tendance à passer au brun. Notez la baïonnette de la carabine.

D1 Le sergent Reynolds portant la veste de patrouille du Service médical de l'Armée et le casque colonial. **D2** Le Commissaire Adjoint Dalton en service, en veste de patrouille, modèle de l'infanterie, et pantalons de petite tenue, avec double bande blanche sur la couture extérieure. **D3** Sergent chef de la garde du drapeau présenté dans la tunique de petite tenue avec les chevrons de la garde du drapeau. **D4** Le Lieutenant Bromhead dans l'habit de serge des autres grades, dépouillé de tous les insignes sauf les écussons de col. **D5** Le Lieutenant Chard présenté avec une tunique de petite tenue et des culottes de cheval. **D6** L'aumônier Smith tendant des munitions d'une musette, dans un manteau civil, noir, long, qui a passé au vert.

E1 Ancien style de la tunique de modèle 1872; en tenue de marche complète; sac à munition noir au lieu de celui en peau plus courant. **E2** Soldat du Génie en tunique de petite tenue avec sacs de modèle d'infanterie. **E3** Soldat de la cavalerie, du Durban mounted rifles, dans l'uniforme coloré avec liseré rouge et ganse noire. **E4** Soldat de la cavalerie, les Stanger mounted rifles, une unité de quarante volontaires qui a servi sous les ordres de la colonne de Pearson.

F1 Soldat, de l'Army Service Corps, en tunique de petite tenue et calot. **F2** Officier, du 91st Highlanders, en tunique de petite tenue, "bottes veld" et ceinturon d'épée de modèle régimentaire. **F3** Sergent en tenue complète de marche. **F4** Tunique de serge, couverture portée en bandéroule et sacs de munitions noirs plutôt qu'en peau à munitions. **F5** Uniforme de petite tenue régimentaire de joueur de cornemuse avec équipement en sac de voyage.

G1 Marin du navire HMS *Boadicea* en pull-over, pantalon et béret blanc, avec un ceinturon brun. **G2** Veste de corvée bleue avec équipement en sac de voyage et sacs à munition noirs. **G3** Les officiers de la Royal Navy semblent avoir eu une préférence pour la veste bleue avec des pantalons bleus ou blancs et la casquette. Ils portaient des révolvers. **G4** Pantalons et pullovers bleus, guêtres de toile et chapeau de paille "sennet". Notez la baïonnette à sabre sur le Martini-Henry.

H1 Veste soutachée en peau de buffle, avec pantalons noirs; il porte une carabine et des bandoulières à cartouches. **H2** Le Lieutenant-Colonel Redvers Buller dans une veste du Norfolk et des culottes de cheval. **H3** Les officiers qui n'appartenaient pas à l'armée régulière préféraient la veste de patrouille de style infanterie avec des culottes de cheval en velours et un chapeau à large bord avec un voile. La plupart d'entre eux étaient armés d'une carabine et d'un révolver. **H4** Soldat de la cavalerie du Frontier Light Horse d'après des photographies d'époque. **H5** De nombreuses unités qui ne faisaient pas partie de l'armée régulière portaient certainement des habits civils avec un voile de couleur autour du chapeau. Le grade de sous-officier est indiqué par le ruban blanc en laine peignée.

I1 Il présente l'étendue complète des modifications de campagne: casque teint, devant de la tunique à plastron inversé et sacs à munitions portés avec le ceinturon de l'épée. **I2** Détails de l'arrière de la tunique et de l'équipement. L'épée est accrochée à un petit crochet sur le ceinturon. **I3** Frith porte la tunique de grande tenue, dont le plastron est inversé, et l'insigne de rang de lieutenant. Le ceinturon en cuir du révolver est porté avec la ceinture à munitions de grande tenue. **I4** Officier en veste de patrouille de la cavalerie pour laquelle le 17th Lancers avait une préférence marquée.

J1 L'Army Hospital Corps semble avoir porté des casques et des calots. Les vestes sont la tunique de petite tenue avec l'écusson distinctif à croix rouge sur le bras droit seulement. **J2** L'uniforme du 21st était principalement le même que celui de l'Infanterie de Ligne mais avec des ganses sur les épaules plutôt que des pattes et l'écusson à grenade sur le col. **J3** Le Colonel Wood porte la tunique de son régiment avec les distinctions de rang de Colonel et un casque teint. **J4** Chelmsford est dans son ensemble de service de combat, une veste de patrouille bleue avec des culottes de cheval et un casque muni d'un voile uni.

K1 Cavalier du Native Horse du Natal dans des vêtements européens et avec un chiffon rouge autour de son chapeau. Il est armé d'une carabine. **K2** Contingent natif du Natal portant la couverture qui lui a été remise et le chiffon rouge autour de la tête, avec un mélange de vêtements européens et africains. Il est équipé de ses propres lance et bouclier. **K3** Ce Souazi porte une coiffure de tête en plumes d'autruches taillées, avec des plumes de sakabuli de chaque côté et des banderoles de plumes sous un bandeau en peau de loutre. Il porte des décorations en queue de vache et une jupe en peau d'animal.

L1 Sergent dans la veste vert sombre et des pantalons noirs du 60th Rifles. Tout l'équipement, y compris la bretelle du fusil est en cuir noir et il porte une épée-baïonnette. **L2** Officier en tunique de petite tenue et casque teint. **L3** Le roi Cetshwayo portant une nappe en guise de manteau et un bâton qui avait appartenu à Shaka. **L4** Les Dragons portaient des sacs à munitions sur leurs ceinturons en campagne ainsi que des ceintures à munitions et une musette. **L5** Major en tunique de grande tenue mais avec ceinture à munitions de petite tenue et ceinturon d'épée.

C1 Quartiermeister mit Feldmütze, blauer Patrouillenjacke mit schwarzem Ledertaschengürtel. **C2** Berittener Infanterist im Regiments-Serge gekleidet mit Kordreithosen; Der Karabiner ist ein Swinburne-Henry. **C3** Lt Col Anthony Durnford RE gekleidet in der Offizierspionier-Patrouillenjacke, Hut mit breiter Krempe und rotem "Puggaree". **C4** Kavallerist der Buffalo Border Guard, eine der Freiwilligeneinheiten von Natal, mit schwarzer Korduniform. **C5** Die Natal-Karabiner trugen blaue Uniformen mit weißen Aufschlägen. **C6** Die berittene Natal-Polizei trug schwarze Uniformen, die im Laufe der Zeit braun wurden. Auffallend ist das Karabiner-Bajonett.

D1 Der Arzt namens Reynolds trug die Patrouillenjacke des Army Medical Department und den Überseehelm. **D2** Der stellvertretende Assistant Commissary Dalton hier mit einer Infanteriepatrouillenjacke und Interimshosen mit doppeltem, weißen Streifen an der Außenseitennaht. **D3** Colour-Sergeant Bourne mit Interimsuniform und Winkelabzeichen eines Colour-Sergeant. **D-** Leutnant Bromhead mit anderem Rang-Serge ohne Insignien, Außer der Kragenabzeichen. **D5** Leutnant Chard mit Interimsgehrock und Reithosen. **D6** Kaplan Smith bei der Ausgabe von Munition aus der Proviantasche. Er ist mit einem langen, schwarzen Zivilmantel bekleidet, der in der Sonne grün verblichen ist.

E1 Gehrock im alten Stil von 1872; mit gesamter Marschausrüstung; schwarze Munitionstasche anstelle der gebräuchlicheren Ochsenledertasche. **E2** Pionier mit Interimsgehrock und im Infanteriemuster gehaltener Tasche. **E3** Kavallerist aus Durban bringt Gewehre in Stellung; er ist in der farbenfrohen Uniform mit roten Verzierungen und schwarzer Litze gekleidet. **E4** Kavallerist Stanger bringt Gewehre in Stellung; eine 40 Mann starke Freiwilligeneinheit diente mit der Pearsonkolonne.

F1 Ein Soldat der Army Service Corps mit Interimsgehrock und Feldmütze. **F2** Offizier der 91st Highlanders mit Interimsgehrock, "Veld-Boots" und Schwertgürtel im Regimentsmuster gehalten. **F3** Sergeant in der gesamten Marschausrüstung gekleidet. **F4** Serge-Gehrock, Decke in banderole und schwarze anstelle der Ochsenledertasche für die Munition. **F5** Interimsuniform des Flötenspielerregiments mit Valise-Ausrüstung.

G1 Matrose der HMS *Boadicea* mit weißem Pullover, Hose und Mütze sowie braunem Gürtel. **G2** Blaue Arbeitsjacke mit Valise-Ausrüstung und schwarzer Munitionstasche. **G3** Offizier der Royal Navy bevorzugten anscheinend die blaue Jacke mit entweder weißen oder blauen Hosen und die Mütze. Revolver wurden getragen. **G4** Blaue Hosen und Pullover, Leinengamaschen und Stroh-"Sennet"-Hüte. Zu beachten ist das Entermesserbajonett an der Martini-Henry.

H1 Lederbraune Jackenlitze mit schwarzen Hosen; er ist mit einem Karabiner bewaffnet und hat Patronengurte. **H2** Lieutenant-Colonel Redvers Buller mit Norfolk-Jacke und Reithosen. **H3** Irreguläre Offiziere bevorzugten die im Infanteriestil gehaltene Patrouillenjacke mit Kordreithosen und Hut mit breiter Krempe sowie "Puggaree". Die Bewaffnung war hauptsächlich ein Karabiner und ein Revolver. **H4** Kavallerist der frontier Light Horse basiert auf Photographien. **H5** Zahlreiche irreguläre Einheiten trugen wahrscheinlich Zivilbekleidung mit farbigen "Puggaree" um die Hüte. Der Rang des NCO war durch das weiße Kammgarnband zu erkennen.

I1 Gezeigt wird der gesamte Umfang der Kampagne-Veränderungen: gefärbter Helm, umgekehrte Brustplattentunika sowie Munitionstaschen mit schwarzem Schwertgürtel. **I2** Rückwärtige Ansicht der Tunika und Ausrüstung. Das Schwert wird an einem kleinen Haken am Schwertgürtel befestigt. **I3** Frith trägt die Tunika mit umgekehrten Brustplatten, sowie Leutnantsrangsinsignie. Lederrevolvergürtel mit vollem Interimstaschengürtel. **I4** Offizier mit der Kavallerie-Patrouillenjacke, die von den 17th Lancer bevorzugt wurde.

J1 Das Army Hospital Corps trug anscheinend Helme und Feldmützen. Die Jacken entstammen dem Interimsgehrock mit einem auffallenden Roten-Kreuz-Abzeichen am rechten Arm. **J2** Die Uniform des 21. Regiments entsprach im großen und ganzen der Line Infantry, hatte aber Schulterkordeln anstelle von Streifen und das Grenadierabzeichen am Kragen. **J3** Colonel Wood trägt den Gehrock seines Regiments mit den Rangabzeichen eines Colonel und einen gefärbten Helm. **J4** Ein Chelmsford befindet sich in seiner Felddienstausrüstung sowie eine blaue Patrouillenjacke mit Reithosen und ein Helm mit einem schlichten "Puggaree".

K1 Ein aus dem Natal stammender Pferdekavallerist mit europäischer Bekleidung, rotem Stoffstreifen um den Hut gewickelt. Er ist mit einem Karabiner bewaffnet. **K2** Das aus dem Natal stammende Kontingent trug die ausgegebenen Decken und roten Stoffstreifen um den Kopf, zusammen mit einer Mischung aus afrikanischer und europäischer Bekleidung. Er ist mit seinem eigenen Speer und Schild bewaffnet. **K3** Dieser Swaze trägt eine Kopfbedeckung aus geschnittenen Straußenfedern und Sakabuli-Federn auf jeder Seite und lange Federbänder unter dem Otterfell-Kopfband. Er ist mit einem Kuhschwanz und Tierfellrock bekleidet.

L1 Sergeant mit dunkler, grüner Gewehrsjacke und schwarzen Hosen der 60th Rifles. Die gesamte Ausrüstung auch die Gewehrschlinge war aus schwarzem Leder hergestellt. Er ist mit einem Schwertbajonett bewaffnet. **L2** Offizier mit Interimsgehrock und gefärbten Helm. **L3** König Cetshwayo trägt eine Tischdecke als Umhang und besitzt einen Stab der Shaka gehörte. **L4** Die Dragoner besaßen Munitionstaschen mit Hüftgürteln in der Kampagne sowie einen Taschengürtel und eine Proviantasche. **L5** Major in Tunika; allerdings mit Interimstaschen- und Schwertgürtel.